CRIMES
THAT SHOCKED
THE WORLD

THE MOST CHILLING TRUE–LIFE STORIES FROM
THE LAST 40 YEARS

CRIMES THAT SHOCKED THE WORLD

DANNY COLLINS

JOHN BLAKE

Published by John Blake Publishing Ltd,
3 Bramber Court, 2 Bramber Road,
London W14 9PB, England

www.johnblakepublishing.co.uk

First published in paperback 2010

ISBN: 978 1 84454 974 0

British Library Cataloguing-in-Publication Data:

A catalogue record for this book is available from the British Library.

Design by www.envydesign.co.uk

Printed in Great Britain by CPI Bookmarque, Croydon CR0 4TD

1 3 5 7 9 10 8 6 4 2

Papers used by John Blake Publishing are natural, recyclable
products made from wood grown in sustainable forests.
The manufacturing processes conform to the environmental
regulations of the country of origin.

All photos © Rex Features

For the victims and their families: eternal peace.

Also by Danny Collins

Nightmare in the Sun
Vanished
The Bloodiest Battles

All published by John Blake Publishing, London

CONTENTS

ACKNOWLEDGEMENTS

Despite its title, this book is not written to shock. It comprises the stories of crimes – some hideous and repellent, some breathtakingly audacious – that have caused the world to pause and take a breath. All were committed within the last 40 years. Some may be fresh in the reader's memory, others may be less well-known, but somewhere, somehow, they made an impact.

In collecting material for this book I studied some unpleasant reports that caused me to seriously reflect on the depth of man's inhumanity to man. The access to these documents, many of which are kept from the public eye in police and security department vaults, was given generously and I thank those authorities for their cooperation. Other sources include police officers, members of the public, colleagues, witnesses to crimes, and the victims themselves. I thank them all. And special thanks to Mrs Jackie Tipping of Hendersen, Nevada, USA, who supplied me with cuttings on the Manson 'Family' and the Sharon Tate and La Bianca murders which she thought might be of interest to me. They were.

As ever, my thanks are also extended to my friends at my publishers, John Blake of London, and the support and advice shown by my indefatigable book editor, John Wordsworth.

My final words of gratitude go to my beautiful wife, Nikki, who reads my manuscripts before tactfully pointing out my more obvious mistakes with a serious expression – although I'm sure she laughs when she leaves the room – and keeps me supplied with Earl Grey tea. The research and any interpretation of the facts are mine. With that said, I must accept all responsibility for any mistakes in the text. They are mine and mine alone, although with respect I would ask you not to shoot the messenger.

Danny Collins
November, 2009
Sierra de Aitana
Spain

FOREWORD

When writing of my investigation into the disappearance of Madeleine McCann in Portugal in 2006 (*Vanished – The Truth About the Disappearance of Madeleine McCann*, John Blake, 2007) I remarked that the genre of true crime writing must, by its very nature, take as its research material the heartbreak and misery inflicted on the victims and family of those involved in the crime – whether as those left with a bitter memory at the loss of a loved one or the shame of a relationship to the perpetrator. That is an unassailable truth.

Each crime brings its own particular horror to the victim and his or her family. A mugging, a burglary or a violent beating are all crimes that leave their mark, physically and mentally, on the victim's psyche. Yet there are crimes that go far beyond the limit of human tolerance and understanding and in so doing scar the psyche of all those who hear of them. Such a crime was that committed by Charles Manson's deranged hippie 'Family' when, in 1969, on his instructions, they broke into a house in Benedict Canyon in the Los Angeles hills and slaughtered five people in a hideous blood bath, even cutting an eight-and-a-half month foetus from the body of victim Sharon Tate, wife of film director Roman Polanski, as she was dangled from a beam across the ceiling. Tate was stabbed many times.

Other victims of that horrific murder spree either shot or stabbed that night were Abigail Folger, heiress to a coffee fortune, celebrity hairstylist Jay Sebring, Polish film director Voitek Frykowski, and 18-year-old Steve Parent, a friend of the house caretaker. Polanski was away in Europe at the time.

On the front door of the house, written in the victims' blood, were the words: 'Death to Pigs'. The next night, wealthy grocer Leno La Bianca and his wife Rosemary, both in their forties, were found stabbed to death in their home across town. A killer had carved the word 'War' on Leno La Bianca's body. The words 'Helter Skelter' were written in blood on the refrigerator.

The Manson crimes are probably among the first that come to mind when one is asked to name the most shocking crime in memory but mankind is so evil that no one act can hold such a title for long. The Manson murders were committed 40 years ago and the horrors are all but lost in the fog of time. Today the crimes are weirder, the execution more horrific, the motives more incomprehensible.

* A two-year-old toddler, beaten with bricks and an iron bar, savaged and left lifeless on a railway track;
* The brutalisation and multiple dual rape of a young couple caught up in a vicious carjacking;

* A depraved killer who sets light to the naked bodies of his schoolgirl victims in a woodland ditch and then joins his victims' parents in the search for the missing girls;

* An Austrian father, obsessed with Nazism, who locks his daughter in a hidden cellar for 24 years, raping his prisoner and disposing of the corpse of one unhealthy issue of his incest by thrusting the body of the one-month-old baby into a furnace in horrific parody of his admired Nazi forbears;

* A serial rapist who suffocates a 15-year-old schoolgirl before the eyes of her schoolfriends who cower away in the darkness as he submits the victim to his lust;

* A murderer who rapes the cold corpses of his victims.

These are all crimes that the human mind reels to accept. They are crimes that defy imagination, that speak of a depravity beyond reason, of such depravity that the world must take note. These are the crimes that almost daily shock our world.

CHAPTER 1

THE MURDER OF JAMES BULGER

Walton, Liverpool, England, 12 February 1993

'C'mon baby, we're going to have some fun'
                                    – John Venables to James Bulger.

There is, in every man and woman on this planet, the capacity for violence – hot and unforgiving when our security or that of our loved ones is breached. But what possesses the cold-blooded killer, he or she who can be moved to commit murder without apparent motive other than an assumed blood lust? What can have moved two ten-year-old boys, no more than children themselves, to lure a younger child from its mother's side and take it to a secluded spot, there to wreak the most horrible violence upon the young body until life was extinguished and then to leave the abused and battered corpse across railway lines in the hope that a passing train would further destroy the body and free the killers of suspicion?

Whereas no one could reasonably deny that Charles Darwin had something when he sat among giant tortoises on the Galapagos Islands and developed his theory of the survival of the fittest, just what being the fittest to survive indicates in this cruel world leaves us much to think about. The obvious, one assumes, is physical strength matched with intelligence in all its varying degrees, but one cannot deny that showing a hint of usefulness or attractiveness to the would-be aggressor must have saved a potential victim on countless occasions.

New-born and very young creatures are certainly not strong enough to fight off an aggressor, therefore they must rely on cuteness and charm to save the day. Puppies are endearing, kittens are cuddly, and children are loveable. All bring out a sense of protectiveness in those around them. Very few men or women would wilfully harm an animal or child without deep moral self recrimination. And yet it happens. Mothers stand by while their drunken boyfriend assaults their child, often with fatal results. Children tie tin cans to a cat's tail and enjoy the animal's frantic efforts to free itself. There is in man a deep, sadistic streak.

Yet sadism in itself has a purpose. It is about domination, self-gratification, and a desire to humiliate. Such motives were evident in the murder of three-year-old James Bulger in a Liverpool suburb in 1993, and the same motives reverberate through every other horrific crime of torture and murder reported in this book. Yet the case of James Bulger reflects a deeper horror in that it was committed by two ten-year-old boys. Animals (if animals will forgive us the description)? Unhinged individuals beyond the salvation offered by Britain's overly moral judicial system? The reader must judge.

The discovery of two-year-old James Patrick Bulger's

tiny bisected, bloodied, and paint-spattered body by a group of bored teenagers wandering beside a seldom-used railway track at Walton, Liverpool, on 14 February 1993, struck horror into the hearts of parents everywhere. Even though he was only a month off his third birthday, so small was James's body that the teenagers first thought that someone had abandoned a doll. The full horror of their discovery on the track alongside the Walton section of the freight line from Edge Hill to Bootle became clear only as they stepped forward for a closer look.

James Bulger had disappeared while shopping with his mother in a shopping centre in Bootle two days earlier. Children often become bored with shopping and wander off to become lost and bewildered among the milling crowd of shoppers, all intent on their own lists of errands. But after two hours of frantic searching by James's parents (Denise and Ralph Bulger), security staff and police, worries of abduction, never far from the minds of all concerned parents, began to surface.

When his mutilated body was examined by investigators, it became obvious that the toddler hadn't wandered onto the track in Walton – two miles from the shopping centre – of his own accord, and the police immediately became aware that they were dealing with a case of violent homicide.

It was clear that James Bulger had been beaten severely, and pathologists would find 38 fractures on his tiny skull, so many that the bone structure had collapsed. The blood-spattered weapons were lying close by in plain view – house bricks and a metre-long iron sleeper tie weighing 10 kg. The child's track bottoms and underclothes had been removed, hinting at a possible dark motive for his abduction and murder. His face, which bore the imprint of a shoe, was stained with blue enamel paint of the type used by model makers, residues of which were also found on his anorak from which the hood had been torn. The hood would later be found high in the branches of a tree along the route from the Strand Shopping Centre to the site where the body was found.

Pathologists concluded that soon after death – caused by any one of the 38 skull fractures – James's body was laid across the railway track in such a position that it would be hit by a passing train. The head and upper body were covered with bricks and rubble to disguise the pathetic form. The motive was clear to investigators – the killer or killers had attempted to make the death of James Bulger appear as a tragic accident.

The horror felt by police investigators and forensic officers was apparent. Who would inflict such injuries on a two-year-old child, beating the victim to death by a deserted railway track? And what could be deduced from the removal of the child's lower clothing? An obvious first assumption would be that they were dealing with a child sex murder. However, that motive would be disproved with the arrest of the killers some weeks later. Ten-year-olds Robert Thompson and Jon Venables revealed they had killed for sadistic pleasure, rather like tying a burning rag to a puppy's tail. They had abducted James Bulger from his mother's side on a whim and, having eventually grown tired of their victim, they had killed him. Then, believing they had artfully covered up the crime, they had gone home for their tea.

On the morning of 12 February 1993, Denise Bulger had taken her son – often called 'Jamie' in the press reports of the murder but never so by his parents and immediate family – to visit his grandmother, Eileen Matthews, in Oak Towers, Kirkby. In fact Eileen had left earlier on a shopping trip to Birkenhead but Denise made the most of their visit by chatting to her sister, Sheila, while James played with his young cousin, Antonia. Later they would be joined by Nicola Bailey, the girlfriend of Denise's brother Paul, who was looking after another Matthews child – a three-year-old cousin of James. Nicola suggested that Denise and James join her and her charge on a shopping expedition to the Strand Shopping Centre in Stanley Road, Bootle town centre.

The ensuing ride in Nicola's Ford Orion delighted James for, like most toddlers, the lively two-year-old loved a car ride and thought it a great adventure. Sadly, the adventure that day was to end in his death.

Meanwhile, Robert Thompson and Jon Venables had left their respective homes in the Liverpool suburbs of Walton and Norris Green that morning with the intention of dodging school for the day, a common enough occurrence among local schoolchildren, referred to generally as 'sagging'. The boys met up and Venables dumped his school bag in an accustomed hiding place where it would stay until he recovered it later. Forgotten in the bag was a note from his mother giving Jon permission to bring home the school gerbils that he was be in charge of for the weekend.

The boys headed for the Bootle Strand Shopping Centre, their usual truancy haunt, where they intended to go on a shoplifting spree for anything that took their fancy.

Just how or when the idea of kidnapping a child came to them was never revealed in questioning, although, typically, the boys blamed each other. Whoever came up with the notion, its purpose was odious: to lure a child into the heavy traffic that roared past the shopping centre to create a potentially fatal accident. But once a victim was in their hands, however, their purpose became even more bloodcurdling.

The pair spent the morning in the shopping centre, generally making a nuisance of themselves by harassing elderly shoppers and stealing from shop displays. Their haul for the morning included sweets, make-up, fruit, Duracell batteries and a small tin of blue enamel paint, similar to the type used in craft modelling. The latter two items were to figure in the crime and the blue enamel paint would prove their downfall.

Throughout the morning, the disruptive presence of Venables and Thompson was noted and later recalled by shop staff and customers. An elderly woman reported being poked and prodded by the boys, who ran off laughing when she remonstrated with them. The staff at McDonald's recalled chasing the boys out of the area where they had been leaping over chairs and throwing leftovers from un-cleared tables. When asked why they weren't in school, the boys replied that it was a holiday. As midday approached, the boys became bored with their antics and began to concentrate on their previously concocted plan to steal a child from under the care of its mother. Thompson and Venables were tired of petty, childish crime and were preparing to step into a new dimension of kidnap and murder.

Their first attempt centred on a three-year-old girl and

her two-year-old brother in the T J Hughes store. Their mother noticed that the girl and her brother were playing with two older boys who were amusing the children by playing chasing games near the door of the shop. She called her children over to her side but a short while later realised they had strayed again. Running outside she saw Venables and Thompson beckoning to the children to follow them and she shouted for them to return. The boys then waved the children away and lost themselves among nearby shoppers. Their plan had gone badly, but with patience other opportunities would soon present themselves.

Meanwhile, James Bulger had become bored with the shopping expedition. His uncle's girlfriend seemed to be taking a long time making up her mind about which underwear to buy and his mother was chatting to a shop assistant. Now he joined his young cousin in chasing up and down between the aisles of clothing in a frenzied game of tag. At one point he became lost among the hanging clothes and, struck with terror, called for his mother. Denise was at his side in an instant and warned him not to stray again.

It was now approaching 1.00 pm and they were all ready for lunch – meat patties, which Denise bought in an adjacent delicatessen. As the children nibbled contentedly at their food, all four moved on to Tesco's where James began to act up again, this time taking items from the shelves and shouting. The final straw was James's attempt to ride an escalator, which led to a paddy tantrum when Denise hauled him off. The only solution seemed to be to bribe the two children with sweets and head for home – but first Denise needed to visit the butcher's to buy something for the family's tea.

Denise was now in a hurry to make her purchases, given James's fractious behaviour and the need to get him home for a sleep, that panacea so favoured by mothers of overactive children. But there was some delay at the counter when the butcher's assistant brought her the wrong chops and she had to wait for them to be changed. When she looked around for James – who had been standing near the door contentedly chewing on his sweets – he was nowhere to be seen.

In a panic, she asked his little cousin where he had gone and the little girl pointed to the arcade outside. 'He went out there,' she told her aunt timidly. Denise rushed outside and frantically tried to spot her diminutive son in his distinctive blue anorak and yellow hood among the milling crowd. Not seeing him, she ran back into the shop and called to Nicola, who was waiting to be served at the cold meat counter. Together they left the shop and began a desperate search, hampered by the presence of the three-year-old girl, who was dragged, bewildered, in their wake. Within a few minutes of James's disappearance, the two women split up and Denise continued unhindered to the security office.

As a message was flashed to shoppers over the Centre's loudspeaker system, Denise began a systematic search of all the shops they had visited previously in the hope that James had wandered back the way they had come. For half an hour she searched in a poorly remembered daze, but to no avail. Nicola Bailey, together with her young charge, was also searching in other directions and questioning passers-by, but no one had seen the little boy. James, it seemed, had disappeared into thin air.

At that moment, James was being led by Jon Venables – later to be seen on the Centre's CCTV holding the toddler by the hand while Robert Thompson walked ahead – out onto Stanley Road. The innocent-looking trio, easily mistaken by passers-by for two young lads and their younger brother, were captured on the camera leaving the shopping centre at 1.42 pm, about the same time that Denise had noticed her son's absence. 'C'mon baby,' said Venables, 'we're going to have some fun.'

In the shopping centre, pandemonium was rife. Police Constable Mandy Walker had arrived in response to a message that a child was missing in the Strand and immediately began to coordinate another search by security officers and other policemen responding to the scene. She also accompanied Denise around the Centre in the hope that the mother would spot her child, pale-faced and panicked, as he searched for his mother. James had been missing now for 40 minutes, and locating a lost child in the Strand usually took no more than 15 minutes. PC Mandy Walker was justifiably concerned.

James was tired. The trio had walked a mile along Stanley Road and his little legs hurt. It was way past his nap time and he was becoming increasingly irritable, a fact that didn't please his kidnappers who were possibly now beginning to regret their impetuous behaviour in snatching the child from under his mother's nose. That had been cool, real grown-up stuff, but the crying toddler was beginning to annoy them.

A passer-by would recall how she saw the two boys with the crying toddler near the canal bank in Stanley

Road and thought the child was 'extremely distressed'. She noticed 'a large bruise' on his forehead, caused, it would later be revealed, when one of the boys had attempted to lift him and dropped him on his head. Unaware of the drama – soon to turn to tragedy – befalling the child, she did not intervene.

In all, the police investigation would reveal that there were 28 sightings of James Bulger with his juvenile kidnappers that day. Although many of the eyewitnesses reported a small child apparently unhappy in the company of two older boys, no one felt compelled to ask why the child was so upset. A motorist driving along Merton Road recalled a child crying as he was pulled along by the arms by two older boys. A woman passing on a bus saw two boys swinging a child by his arms. The child, she reported, was alternately laughing and crying. She identified the boys as about nine years old. The child, she told police, was 'just a baby'.

By the time Thompson and Venables had reached the raised, grassed-over site of the Breeze Hill Reservoir it was about 4.20 pm, approximately around the same time police were alerted to James's disappearance by Strand security staff. The boys with their tiny victim in tow then left the reservoir area and turned into nearby Stuart Street, which they followed to its junction with County Road, a busy main route out of the city that would eventually bring them to the scene of James's eventual murder at Walton. Did they have a goal in mind? Neither has ever said if the route was planned.

James was becoming more irritable and tired. They were now nearly two miles from the Strand Shopping Centre, a long way for a two-year-old to walk. His distressed behaviour was attracting the attention of more and more eyewitnesses who would come forward after the body was discovered to tell investigators varying stories of a sobbing toddler and his two 'brothers'. But again, nobody intervened. It is not in the English nature to enquire too deeply of a spectacle witnessed in the street. Look no further than how abusive thugs on public transport are ignored as commuters become deeply involved behind their newspapers.

Back in Kirkby, the news of James's disappearance began to circulate among the Bulger and the Matthews clans, and the menfolk started to tour the area around the Strand in their cars, looking for the child. By now consumed by guilt, Denise wept as she was comforted by the womenfolk. 'You can't watch them forever,' was a constant phrase given in assurance to the distressed mother. How far could a two-year-old have gone, after all? He'd be found curled up asleep somewhere – of course he would.

On the way to Walton, Jon Venables had grabbed James's anorak by the hood and attempted to drag the child along. The material tore and, giving the fallen toddler a kick to get him to his feet, Venables hurled the hood into the branches of a tree where it would later be recovered by police. Finally, the duo and their victim arrived at the site of the old Walton railway station which had been demolished following the conversion of the old passenger line to freight. Low brick walls on either side of the double track still mark the original sites of the passenger platforms. It was here that the final torment of little James Bulger began. Throughout their statements to police following their arrests, neither boy would admit to physically harming the toddler and laid the blame for each injury firmly against the other.

What is evident from forensic and Scene of Crime reports is that James Bulger was used as a target for house bricks, beaten about the head and body with wooden sticks and an iron tie bar, and stripped of his underclothes. An attempt, never confirmed by police who remained silent on many of the toddler's more severe injuries, was possibly made to jam batteries into his anus. He was also spattered with blue enamel paint, a residue of which would be found on Venables's jacket following his arrest three weeks later.

Robert Thompson and Jon Venables were tried for the abduction and murder of James Patrick Bulger at Preston Crown Court on 1 November, 1993. Both boys had turned 11 by the date of the trial but were still, nonetheless – along with 10-year-old Mary Bell in 1968 – the youngest children to stand trial for murder in Britain in the 20th century.

English law dictates that children between 10 and 14 are exempt from criminal responsibility unless the prosecution can prove that at the time of the offence the child was aware of the gravity of the crime. Thus, the jury was faced with deciding whether Thompson and Venables were equally guilty of the offences with which they were charged.

In the late morning of 24 November, after counsels' closing speeches, the jury retired to consider its verdict and returned just under six hours later to pronounce both defendants guilty as charged on all counts. On passing his sentence that both should be detained during Her Majesty's Pleasure, Justice Morland told the young murderers: 'The killing of James Bulger was an act of unparalleled evil and barbarity. This child of two was taken from his mother on a journey of over two miles, and then on a railway line battered to death without mercy. Then his body was placed across the railway line so that it would be run over by a train, in an attempt to conceal the murder. In my judgement your conduct was both cunning and very wicked.'

AFTERNOTE

Jon Venables and Robert Thompson were sentenced to be detained at Her Majesty's Pleasure for a minimum of eight years. In response to public opinion, the incumbent Home Secretary, Michael Howard, attempted to change the minimum time served to 15 years but this was rebutted by the European Court of Appeal. Venables and Thompson were released on a life licence in 2001 and given new identities after serving the eight years minimum tariff set by the trial judge. An injunction made at the time and still in force prevents their new identities or whereabouts being published.

CHAPTER 2

DEATH ON CHIPMAN STREET

Knoxville, Tennessee, USA 6 January 2007

> *'I've just got to take out the trash'*
> — Lemaricus Davidson, after placing his
> victim's body in a garbage bin.

Hugh Christopher (Chris) Newsom Jr and Channon Christian were a wholesome couple. He was a 23-year-old former baseball player for the Halls High School Red Devils who had graduated in 2002 and was currently working as a trim carpenter in Knoxville, Tennessee, the town where he had grown up. He met his girlfriend Channon Christian – a graduate of Farragut High School and a senior majoring in sociology at the University of Tennessee – when the Christian family moved to Knoxville from their native Louisiana in 1997.

The couple had met as teenagers on a social evening and Channon had fallen in love with the slender youth, admiring his prowess on the baseball pitch and responding to his ready smile. Her feelings were reciprocated and both

15

sets of parents felt that an engagement might ensue, not too far in the future, perhaps when Channon had completed her sociology degree. There was no doubt that the attractive blue-eyed blonde had captured Chris Newsom's heart.

On 6 January the couple drove in Channon's almost new Toyota 4 Runner to watch an outdoor movie at Market Square – a common distraction in Knoxville provided courtesy of the Knox County Library. Afterwards they had dinner in a local restaurant before visiting friends in the town's Washington Heights Apartments, saying their farewells just after midnight for the drive home. They never arrived.

Despite being the largest city in East Tennessee and ranking third largest in the state, Knoxville's population is slightly less than 180,000 souls. Outside the city nucleus the area is mostly agricultural. People usually get where they're going and the incidence of road traffic accidents is minimal.

Chris's and Channon's parents – Gary and Deena Christian and Hugh and Mary Newsom – were puzzled to find their respective offsprings' beds un-slept in the next morning and hurriedly rang each other to confirm whether the couple had slept at each other's parents' home. But it was clear that the couple had never returned to either property. Channon Christian and Christopher Newsom had disappeared within minutes of leaving the house of the friends they had visited the previous evening. Their worried parents called the police and immediate checks were carried out at hospitals and with local traffic police. Chief of Police Sterling Owen directed the search for the young couple and speculation was rife about their disappearance. Both Channon and Christopher were known as level-headed individuals with their lives and future clearly mapped out. A runaway elopement was discounted and anxiety grew for their safety.

Later that afternoon, that anxiety became reality when the brutalised and burned body of a young white male was found in East Knoxville near a section of railway tracks between the Cherry Street and Ninth Avenue bridges. It was identified by a police officer who knew the family of Christopher Newsom Jr. 'I recognised him by his eyes,' the officer told Chris's father. The 23-year-old baseball star had been shot in the head, spine, and lower body. His hands were bound behind him. An examination of the bloodied corpse in situ revealed even more horrifying details. Christopher's penis had been savagely hacked off and his body showed signs of repeated anal rape, later confirmed by autopsy. Whoever had dumped him near the tracks had soaked his body in gasoline and set it on fire before leaving the scene.

The search for Channon grew in intensity. Meanwhile, her parents returned to the police with her cellphone number and a trace run by the service providers led to the discovery of her abandoned vehicle in the rural neighbourhood of Chipman Street the next day. The vehicle was searched and fingerprints sent for comparison to the National Index. When the results arrived a few days later, prints found on an envelope containing Channon's bank statement found inside the Toyota SUV led police to 2316 Chipman Street, a clapboard single storey home not far from where the vehicle was found. It was the residence of 25-year-old

Lemaricus Devall 'Slim' Davidson, a local black petty criminal with a long rap sheet of violent robbery and carjacking offences. Davidson was nowhere to be seen and the house appeared to be unoccupied.

A search warrant for the house was executed on the following day and revealed some broken sticks of furniture, a .22 calibre revolver and a .22 rifle. In the kitchen a horrific discovery awaited. Police found Channon Christian's body crammed inside a large domestic trash can, covered with plastic sheets. An autopsy would reveal that the young student had died of asphyxiation. An all-points, stop-and-detain warrant was issued for Davidson, who eventually surrendered to police. He was arrested on suspicion of murder and his subsequent questioning by investigators led to the arrests of three other black men and one woman: Davidson's half brother Letalvis 'Rome' Cobbins (24), George Geovonni 'Detroit' Thomas (27), Eric DeWayne 'E' Boyd (34) and 18-year-old Vanessa Coleman who, Davidson told police, had all been visiting him from Kentucky on the day of the carjacking. All were eventually charged with various counts of rape, murder, and hijacking.

Lemaricus Davidson would later claim that his stepbrother, Cobbins, together with Thomas and Boyd had carjacked the couple after he had told Cobbins that he and his friends from Kentucky were freeloading on his hospitality. He claimed never to have seen Newsom and pointed his finger at Cobbins and Thomas for the victims' rape and murder. He admitted seeing Channon Christian brought into the house and noted that she was wearing a 'hoodie' and had not been blindfolded. 'That meant they'd have to kill her 'cos she'd seen faces,' he told police and federal investigators. 'I took the keys of the girl's car from my brother and drove away. I didn't want to see what was going to happen.'

He claimed never to have returned to the scene, although his testimony would change dramatically at trial. Although Davidson's defence team would later offer up Cobbins as the ringleader and the chief protagonist in the multiple rape and murder of Channon, irrefutable DNA evidence pointed to Davidson's fingerprints and semen as proof that he took an active part in her rape and death.

The details of the crime, together with the horrific injuries inflicted on the couple before death, drove the press into a feeding frenzy. The case had all the hallmarks of racial ferment. The murdered couple were white and middle class while their attackers and killers were known black criminals. As sensationalised press reports recorded the agonies of the victims, Tennessee reeled in shock. Gradually the full horror of the young lovers' deaths was revealed under questioning as each suspect fought to lay the blame on each other. Seeking immunity from the public prosecutor, Vanessa Coleman told investigators that she was present when Davidson led Channon blindfolded with her hands tied behind her, into the room and snapped her neck from behind. He then wrapped the body in garbage bags and stuffed it into the bin, making a remark about 'taking out the trash'. She also alleged that George Thomas had told her he 'felt bad' about the death of Chris Newsom, whom he had raped and mutilated along with Cobbins before the latter shot him to death after marching him to the railway tracks opposite the house. Thomas allegedly then poured gasoline over the corpse and set it ablaze.

The story finally put together by police was that after hijacking Channon Christian's Toyota SUV from Washington Heights at gunpoint, the attackers had bound the couple in the back seat and taken them to Davidson's residence in Chipman Street, where Channon was forced to watch as the men repeatedly raped Newsom – court records refer to 20 counts of rape committed on the couple – then hacked off his penis, shot him multiple times and dragged his corpse along to the nearby railway track between Cherry Street and Ninth Avenue, where they set it on fire.

With Newson out of the way, the perpetrators next focused their depraved sadism on the terrified Channon. While not clear whether the 21-year-old student was killed within hours or kept alive until the following day, it was evident that she suffered agonies as she was gang-raped numerous times, beaten almost to the point of death, had a breast cut from her conscious body, and urinated upon. At some time one of the gang, possibly Vanessa Coleman, raped her both vaginally and anally with a broken chair leg.

The sheer depravity of the attacks is difficult to comprehend. Why, with a woman victim in their power, did the men resort to the repeated anal rape of their male victim? The answer may lie in that all the men arrested had served prison sentences where male rape is common – Cobbins had finished serving a six-year sentence only five months before – and may have developed a taste for that particular depravity. Some psychologists interviewed for this book believed it possible that Newsom may have angered his attackers or provoked them to the point where they showed their contempt and dominance of a 'little white boy' by raping him in front of his girlfriend. Whatever the reasons, Christopher Newsom's pain and torment were over, and now the gang turned its evil on the helpless Channon.

Investigators still remain unclear whether Channon Christian was held and tortured for two days following the murder of Christopher Newsom or whether she died the next day. Certainly, when her corpse was discovered it was apparent that raw bleach had been poured down her throat and used to scrub her mutilated body. This, forensic pathologists decided, could have taken place post mortem and was done to destroy DNA evidence. There is no doubt, however, that Channon Christian met her death by suffocation after being bound inside several plastic garbage bags and stuffed into the large garbage bin inside the house, where her body was discovered by police. A policeman remarked: 'She died with her eyes open.' If Coleman's account is to be believed, Channon may have merely fainted when Davidson attempted to break her neck. She recalls Davidson asking her if the girl was dead, to which she claims to have retorted, 'Look yourself, Bro, I 'ain't no nurse.'

With the sensational press coverage, the case had now become a *cause célèbre* for black activists and white supremacists alike. In May 2007, 30 white supremacists demonstrated in downtown Knoxville in protest at the murders and questions were asked in the right wing press regarding the absence of comments on the case by the Reverends Al Sharpton and Jesse Jackson, both well known for their outspoken deliveries on the issues of race.

Perhaps they felt there was no infringement of black civil rights involved, but their reluctance to speak to the press about the murders was noted.

All those arrested were charged with the murders of Hugh Christopher Newsom Jr and Channon Christian, and with other charges relative to the crime. Davidson, Cobbins, and Thomas were all indicted by a Grand Jury on a total of 46 counts each: these were 16 counts of felony murder, two counts of premeditated murder, two counts of especially aggravated robbery, four counts of especially aggravated kidnapping, 20 counts of aggravated rape, and two counts of theft. Eric DeWayne 'E' Boyd was not indicted for murder and faced only federal charges as an accessory after the fact. He was eventually convicted in federal court of being an accessory to the carjacking and was sentenced to 18 years in prison. The prosecution reserved the right to bring him to trial on capital murder charges following evidence gathered in the trials of Cobbins, Davidson, and Coleman. Pre-trial proceedings were scheduled for July 2009.

It should be clarified that in each indictment the large number of counts of rape were not included to reflect the number of rapes that actually occurred, but to provide a range of options for the prosecutors, although without doubt the victims were both sexually abused a number of times before their murders.

On 25 August 2009, Letalvis 'Rome' Cobbins (24) was found guilty of multiple counts of first degree and felony murder in the death of Channon Christian but opted for lesser charges of facilitating murder in the killing of Newsom. He was also convicted of rape, kidnapping, and robbery, charges that carry the weight of 15 to 25 years' imprisonment. Cobbins was found guilty on 33 of the 38 counts against him but the jury baulked at calling for his death and sentenced him to life imprisonment without parole. He narrowly escaped paying the ultimate price for his crimes. District Attorney Randy Nichols had announced that the state would be seeking the death penalty for Cobbins, Davidson and Coleman, if convicted.

Meanwhile, the defence attorneys of Lemaricus Devall 'Slim' Davidson pleaded that publicity against the accused would require a change of venue in order to ensure a fair trial. The motion was subsequently denied by the presiding judge as premature, although it was clear that Davidson's eventual conviction following the denied request for a change of venue would lead, in the case of a guilty verdict, to the filing of an appeal on the grounds of jury prejudice.

That prejudice, if it had existed, wouldn't have been enough for the families of the victims. Gary Christian, father of Channon, had to be physically restrained when Cobbins told the court that Channon had offered him oral sex in return for his help in escaping. Cobbins's extraordinary statement was made when, against his attorneys' advice, he took the stand to testify on his own behalf. Before Cobbins began his testimony, Judge Baumgartner dismissed a motion by his two reluctant court-appointed defence attorneys, Kim Parton and Scott Green, to withdraw from the case citing client/counsel differences.

Cobbins's testimony was a blatant effort to place the blame for the crime on his fellow conspirators, referred to in court as the 'Kentucky Crowd', while making himself appear as a man struggling with a moral dilemma during the assaults on Newsom and Christian, unable to intervene for fear of his life. He told the court that he, his girlfriend Vanessa Coleman, and Thomas had come from Kentucky to spend the New Year 2007 with his brother Davidson, who he hadn't seen for years due to regular spells of imprisonment. Davidson had been delighted to see him and suggested they go together to Washington Ridge Apartments to meet a girlfriend of Davidson. According to Cobbins, Eric Boyd – who had already been found guilty and sentenced as an accessory in the case, accompanied them.

The trio smoked marijuana on the way to the apartments and there spotted Newsom and Christian hugging and kissing in a Toyota SUV. Davidson and Boyd jumped out and carjacked them at pistol point. At this point Cobbins insisted that he wanted nothing to do with the carjacking but Davidson insisted he follow them back to Davidson's house on Chipman Street. He told the court that all four suspects were at the house when he, Davidson, and Boyd arrived with Newsom and Christian and that he had told Coleman and Thomas that the three of them should leave because of what was going on, but, in his words, 'that never happened'. When he told Davidson of their intention, his brother produced a gun and threatened to shoot anyone who attempted to leave the house.

Throughout his testimony Cobbins made no mention of the rape and murder of Christopher Newsom, only recalling that Davidson and Thomas came back into the house for a while, left about half an hour later and returned with 'dark stains' on their shirts when they returned the second time. His inflammatory statement that so riled the father of Channon related to when he told the court that he had gone into the bedroom where Channon was bound on the bed and untied her bonds so that she could drink some of the water he had brought her.

At that point, according to Cobbins, the young woman offered him oral sex if he would convince Davidson to let her go. He claimed he accepted her offer and told the stunned jury he heard 'noises that concerned him' as he ejaculated. At that point the victim's mother struggled to restrain her husband from attacking Cobbins. Cobbins was found guilty on 33 counts, including first degree felony murder, first degree premeditated murder, especially aggravated robbery, especially aggravated kidnapping with a weapon, aggravated rape with a weapon, aggravated rape with bodily injury, aggravated rape while aided by others, and theft of property.

He was found not guilty on five counts, including the murder of Newsom during his rape, the murder of Christian during Newsom's rape, and three counts of aggravated rape of Newsom. The trial of Cobbins's half brother Lemaricus Davidson began on 19 October 2009, with that of Vanessa Coleman and George Thomas to follow. Davidson's defence strategy was to accuse Cobbins of lying about his and Davidson's role with regard to the carjacking, rapes, and murders. However, his attorneys, Doug Trant and David Aldridge, presented a story very similar to that of Cobbins to explain the presence of their client's semen on the dead girl.

According to Davidson, Christian had offered him vaginal sex in return for her life. It was a flawed tactic since, even if it had been believed, it could only have presented the picture of a terrified girl begging for her life and willing to make any sacrifice to escape death. It failed to save Davidson and on 28 October he was found guilty on all counts. On 30 October the jury imposed the death sentence for his role as ringleader in the killings.

Although no information was available at the time this book went to publication, there was no doubt in Davidson's defence strategy that room had been left for the manoeuvre of appeal. Criminals sentenced to death in the USA may spend decades on Death Row while their anti-capital punishment lawyers, often working pro bono, bring repeated appeals for stays of executions to keep their clients away from lethal injection.

The appeal process in the United States is long, following a trail through various stages of hearings as far as the Federal Supreme Court, where an unfavourable decision leaves only a plea of clemency, seldom granted, to the state governor. Tennessee's state governor is Phil Bredesen, a free-thinking Democrat hard on drugs and crime and a staunch supporter of family values. Of late, the Anti-Terrorism and Effective Death Penalty Act (AEDPA), passed by President Bill Clinton in 1996, has severely constrained the time limit for appeal and the conditions under which an appeal can be heard.

The trial of George Geovonni Thomas was set for 1 December. The defence of Vanessa Coleman – who in her haste to condemn everyone but herself had made incriminating statements before counsel was appointed or a plea bargain arranged – had appealed a key ruling over immunity and no trial date had been set.

The murder house at 2316 Chipman Street was bought in October 2008 by Waste Collections Inc, the company that owned the adjoining land, and the house was demolished. In its place a memorial was erected to Channon Christian and Hugh Christopher Newsom Jr, victims of the horrors of a fatal carjacking one night in Knoxville, Tennessee, that went far beyond the limits of human understanding.

CHAPTER 3

SALLY ANNE BOWMAN

South Croydon, London, England, September 2005

'I want to be the next Kate Moss'
– aspiring teenage model Sally Anne Bowman in 2003.

The murder of Sally Anne Bowman in the London suburb of Croydon on September 2005 shocked a nation which was becoming increasingly blasé about horrific street slayings. Young men died bleeding from savage knife wounds after a pointless argument; children at play were snatched off the street to be sexually used and abused until their young lives were choked out of them by a pervert's hand; street muggings were frequent and almost not to be remarked on; old age pensioners were beaten in their homes and died for the meagre content of their purses; football matches ended in a welter of missiles and café tables.

Yet the murder of Sally Anne Bowman, a young and aspiring model, was so horrific in its execution and the indignities committed on her body so repellent that everyone who heard of it sat up and took notice. And ironically and dramatically, for all the perpetrated horror and violence of that night it was a minor brawl about soccer that brought her killer to justice.

Those who knew Sally Anne during her short life would describe her as an enigmatic 18-year-old, in varying degrees opinionated, warm, argumentative, and naïve. The latter quality was possibly that which cost Sally Anne her life, although her refusal to be intimidated by the actions of a man whom she dismissed to her friends and employer as a 'wacko' would also be a contributory factor.

Sally Anne Bowman was born in South Croydon – at the time a part of the county of Surrey but now classified as a suburb of London's sprawl – on 11 September 1987, the youngest of four sisters. Her early school years were spent at Cheam Fields Primary School in nearby Sutton, she moved on to Cheam High and later attended the British Record Industry Trust School of Performing Arts and Technology in Croydon. Pursuing her dream to follow another Croydon girl, the model Kate Moss, onto the cover of *Vogue*, at the age of 16 she joined the local Pulse Model Management Agency and worked on the London catwalks, including the Café de Paris on Piccadilly and the Swatch Alternative Fashion Week. Tall, willowy, with long blonde hair and large blue eyes, the budding model, although hardly out of school, was fiercely ambitious and could not wait to break into the big time.

Unfortunately for Sally Anne, she had also attracted the attention of Mark Dixie, a 36-year-old pub chef, who was into both drug and alcohol abuse, and who frequented many of the dance clubs and pubs in Croydon town centre where Sally Anne often went with her sisters. Dixie began to stalk his victim, showing up at karaoke nights where Sally Anne, a proficient singer, liked to perform her favourite songs – Bette Midler's 'Wind Beneath My Wings' and Celine Dion's 'Love Goes On', the theme from *Titanic*.

On one occasion he even turned up at the hairdressing salon where she worked and insisted that 'the tall blonde one' washed and cut his hair. It's possible that Dixie's obsession had given Sally Anne cause for unease, since her relatives told police that three or four days before her murder she seemed worried and unsettled.

The night of Saturday 24 September 2005 was to evolve into a blood bath of horror but it started innocently enough when Sally Anne and her 22-year-old sister Nicole went into Croydon to visit a club. Nicole decided to go home early while Sally Anne stayed for a drink with friends at a nearby bar before telephoning her on/off boyfriend, 22-year-old plasterer Lewis Sproston, to ask him to give her a lift to her newly-rented apartment in Blenheim Crescent.

It was the first time in 30 days that Sally Anne had returned to the apartment, having spent most of this time back home with her mother, Linda, and sisters during a bout of homesickness and worry over grocery bills – common enough in young women who leave home to demonstrate their newfound independence.

Lewis arrived reluctantly, annoyed because Sally Anne had chosen to go out without him that evening but was now treating him as a taxi driver. He found himself in the quandary that can affect all young men in a state of unrequited love towards offhand young women they have known since schooldays and who go on to seemingly glamorous careers in modelling or show business. Sally Anne, meanwhile, while being aware of the dismissive way she often treated him, was nonetheless jealous at the thought of him seeing other women, and the couple's relationship was in a continuous state of flux.

As usual they argued at length and it wasn't until 4.10 am that Sally Anne climbed out of the car and Lewis drove away in a temper, neglecting to escort Sally Anne to her door, less than 50 metres away. It was an action, he would later recall, that he would regret and that would stay with him for the rest of his life. As the sound of the car faded into the night and as Sally Anne reached the drive of 26 Blenheim Crescent, a figure lurched out at her from behind a skip.

Sally Anne Bowman's semi-nude body was found by a neighbour walking her dog just over two hours later. Some residents of Blenheim Crescent would later recall hearing a young woman's screams at around 4.15 am but, as reluctant as neighbours always are to leave their beds in the middle of the night, apart from a glance out of the window into the darkness, no one investigated further.

The dog-walker noticed the bare legs of a woman protruding from behind a skip and a cluster of wheelie bins on the drive of number 26. Lying face up behind the skip in a pool of blood was the body of Sally Anne, dead from loss of blood caused by seven savage knife wounds to the neck, abdomen, and lower body. Forensic pathologists summoned to the scene would discover that three of the wounds had been inflicted with such force that the knife blade had passed clean through the body.

They would also register that her lower undergarments had been removed and her short denim skirt had been bunched up around her waist. Sally's sleeved white crop top had been pulled up to her waist and bite marks to the neck, stomach, and right breast suggested a frenzied sexual attack, either before or during death. The body had been partially covered with dust and cement from the skip and the presence of other body fluids indicated a savage resentment on the part of the perpetrator against the victim. Whoever had committed those atrocities on the young model had boiled with hatred and madness during their execution.

The first senior police officer on the scene was Detective Superintendent Stuart Clundy who, as a father of two young daughters, was shocked and repulsed by what he saw. Such savagery was so unusual in a rape, and the veteran detective knew instinctively that he was searching for an obsessed character who had offended before. Such bestiality could only be rooted in a deranged personality.

Sally Anne's mother, Linda, recalled hearing of her daughter's death from DC Steve Martin who arrived at the Bowman home with two women PCs. Linda's screams brought her daughter Nicole running down from upstairs to hear the detective's solemn words. With a whimper, Nicole crumpled to the floor. She had last seen her younger sibling fit and well in Croydon town centre at around 2.00 am when she left to come home alone. Now her baby sister was dead. Sally Anne had died of massive exsanguination, a rapid loss of blood clinically termed as hypervolemia. So rapid was the blood loss that she had died within minutes of the attack.

Missing from the crime scene were Sally Anne's mobile phone and white Prada handbag containing her purse, make-up, and passport. A chain and pendant had been wrenched from her neck and the killer had cut off a hank of blonde hair as the girl lay dead or dying. An earring had also been torn from her right ear. But in his haste and fury of lust the killer had left many clues before he fled. Sally Anne's body and the crime scene yielded bite casts, saliva, semen, hairs – each a telling clue for the investigators who would now work to track down the killer.

The first and most obvious suspect was her ex-boyfriend, Lewis Sproston. As in any murder investigation the prime suspect is always the person known to have been the last person to see the victim alive. At first sight, things did not look good for Sproston. He admitted being with Sally Anne up to 4.10 am, just before the time when neighbours in Blenheim Crescent had heard a young woman screaming, and there were many witnesses to the fact that the couple were prone to argue forcibly, on more than one occasion so noisily that police had been called to intervene. In a statement to police he also admitted sending Sally Anne a text message before he left to pick her up in Croydon to the effect that if he saw her with another man when he arrived he would 'spit on her' in public. Marks on his neck also showed where, during an argument in the car, Sally Anne had grabbed him around the neck so violently that a silver chain had been broken and pulled from his throat.

So certain was Sproston that the argument had been loud enough to wake neighbours that he asked police who came to question him on the morning of the murder and before he was told of her death: 'Is this about the row with Sally Anne last night?' Sproston's only recollection of another person in Blenheim Crescent that Sunday morning was of a man who had approached the car while he sat talking with Sally Anne and who had glared aggressively at the couple through the windscreen. He had made to get out of the car to confront the man but Sally Anne had stopped him, probably fearing that in his current ill temper he and the Peeping Tom might come to blows. The man had then turned and walked away and they had thought no more about it. Sproston was held for 72 hours while the interrogation continued but, as Superintendent Stuart Clundy admitted in a later interview with the press, 'It was obvious the lad was telling the truth and we would have to look elsewhere.'

Armed with such a battery of DNA evidence taken from the scene and gathered at autopsy, police began a search of DNA databases in the hope of trapping the killer. Investigators were convinced that they were hunting a serial rapist who, once having stepped into the dark shadow of death would not hesitate to kill again. Criminal profilers brought in to the case were also convinced that Sally Anne Bowman's murder was an escalation in violence on behalf of a mentally unstable, sex-obsessed individual who probably acted under the influence of drink and/or drugs. Unbeknown to them, the man they were seeking fitted the profile perfectly.

A report had already arrived on Superintendent Clundy's desk of a knife attack on a woman in Sanderstead Road at around 3.00 am on 25 September, a mere mile away, and an hour before Sally Anne's screams were heard in Blenheim Crescent. The woman described a squat man of medium build brandishing a knife, who had asked her for money and oddly apologised before slashing her across the face. He had run off when surprised by an approaching taxi. No DNA was gathered from the scene but a surprise hit linked the Blenheim Crescent DNA with that of a serious sexual assault that had occurred in nearby Purley Cross when an unidentified man masturbated and ejaculated over a woman in a telephone kiosk in 2001.

Investigators now knew their quarry was local and immediately launched a DNA screening of 4000 men in the area where Sally Anne had died and 1700 local men also responded to a call to attend a DNA screening centre in South Croydon. But police were aware that thousands of males in South Croydon's estimated 250,000 population were still unchecked.

An e-fit of the 2001 Purley sex attacker, whose DNA linked the perpetrator to Sally Anne's murder, was released and police reported that 350 potential suspects had been questioned during their enquiries, with a special emphasis put on the search for a former customer of the Blast Hair Designs hairdressing salon in Kenley, Surrey, where Sally Anne had worked. The man had spoken with an Australian accent.

As months went by more details emerged about the case – it now appeared that the killer had felt confident enough to return to Sally Anne's body after the stabbing to take photographs of her corpse with a mobile phone. Then a major breakthrough came when police in Crawley, Sussex, were called to a brawl following a World Cup match. One man in particular had become extremely distressed when told he must give a DNA sample. Once compared with other DNA samples on the police database it became clear why: the sample was an exact match to those left at the Blenheim Crescent crime scene. The man was 35-year-old Mark Dixie and he spoke with an Australian accent. The date was 27 June 2006, almost nine months to the day that Sally Anne Bowman was murdered and raped in South Croydon.

At the time of his arrest Mark Phillip Dixie, born in Streatham, London, on 25 September 1970, worked at Ye Old Six Bells pub in Horley, Surrey, close to Gatwick Airport. His acquired Australian accent came from his time working as a pub cook in Australia between 1993 and 1999. He was deported back to the UK on visa offences after being found guilty of exposing himself and making sexual demands to a female jogger. A criminal records check revealed that Mark Dixie had a violent criminal history with 16 recorded sex attacks on women in both Australia and the UK. However, only since 2004 does the law in the UK allow arresting officers to take involuntary DNA swabs from suspects arrested in any circumstances.

Following Dixie's conviction for the Bowman murder in February 2007, Detective Superintendent Clundy called publicly for the creation of a national DNA database, claiming that if such a directory had existed in September 2005, Sally Anne's killer would have been in custody within days of her death.

At the time of Sally Anne's murder, Dixie, an absentee father of three, was often seen in the clubs and bars of Croydon town centre. He had lodgings in Avondale Road, South Croydon, just a few miles from Sally's family home and her apartment in Blenheim Crescent. Dixie was familiar with Blenheim Crescent, having lived there with a girlfriend, the mother of his third child, two years previously. It would later be discovered that Western

Australian police in Perth also had the DNA profile of Mark Dixie collected in the unsolved case of the rape and attempted murder of a Thai student in 1998. In a scenario startlingly similar to the murder of Sally Anne Bowman, the student was stabbed several times by a masked man and raped while she was unconscious. The information was revealed after the Metropolitan Police asked their Australian counterparts to re-examine any unsolved murder cases involving rape that might be linked to Dixie. Other evidence came to light of a sexual assault upon a British woman in a lift in 1989.

It was becoming clear that DNA evidence had trapped a very dangerous serial sexual offender whose use of violence to gain control over his victims had finally resulted in murder. There was no doubt in the investigators' minds that Mark Dixie was primed to kill again and would have done so if not detained due to a minor brawl that allowed arresting officers to mandatorily take a sample of his DNA.

At his trial in February 2008 at the Old Bailey, the cocky, smirking Dixie astounded the court by offering the defence that he did not kill Sally Anne but had stumbled across her body by chance while out walking after a drink and drugs session with friends Vicky Chandler and Diane Glassborow in Croydon to celebrate his 35th birthday. Dixie claimed he was wandering aimlessly when he noticed the half-naked corpse of the murdered girl lying in the drive of 26 Blenheim Crescent and, high on cocaine, he 'took advantage of the situation'. Showing no emotion, Dixie continued: 'When I realised she was dead I put bits of concrete from a nearby skip into her mouth and on her body because I hoped it would hide my DNA, then I ran to a friend's flat a few streets away in South Croydon.'

Dixie had returned to Avondale Road, where he was lodging at the time.

Mark Dixie had failed to impress the jury, who took just three-and-a-half hours to find him guilty on all counts. Sentencing him to life imprisonment with a minimum of 34 years, Judge Gerald Gordon told him: 'I shall only say what you did that night was so awful and repulsive that I do not propose to repeat it. Your consequent conduct shows you had not the slightest remorse for what you had done.' A year later a panel of three Court of Appeal judges found an application to appeal lodged by Dixie's solicitors MacLaverty Cooper Atkins of Kingston 'entirely without merit'.

CHAPTER 4

MASSACRE IN SREBRENICA

Bosnia and Herzegovina, July 1995

'I do not know how Mr Krajišnik or Mr Karadžić will explain that to the world. That is genocide'
— General Ratko Mladić, on receiving his orders to eliminate the Muslim population.

When Slovenia and Croatia declared their sovereignty in 1991 it was clear to political observers that Yugoslavia was about to fall apart. Fighting began almost immediately as the new republics voiced their independence from Yugoslavia, where ethnic hatred had festered during the 46 years of enforced national republicanism under Marshal Tito. It was the beginning of the bloodiest war of attrition in Europe since World War II. The result was a bitter conflict between the main ethnic groups of Serbs, Croats, and Slovenes as the competing nationalisms found the territory too small to be divided between the three.

Hatreds that had festered since 1945 between the Croats

and Serbs – when the fascist Usta?e sought to create an ethnically pure Croatian state entailing the elimination of all Serbian and Muslim minorities in Croatia – rapidly rose to the surface. They found a ready home in the minds of ethnic groups manipulated by those who sought to gain power and prominence as nationalist leaders, such as Serbian power-players Ante Pavić Franjo Tudjman, and Slobodan Milosević. The latter had risen to the presidency of Serbia and Yugoslavia and of the Social Republic of Serbia and Federal Serbia in 1987; Radovan Karadžić was a family doctor until he was elected to the presidency of the Republika Srpska in 1992.

The first to break away from the disintegrating Yugoslavia was Slovenia. Its departure occurred with little incident and the new republic was recognised as an independent state by the United Nations and European Community in 1992. Slovenia joined NATO and the European Union in 2004. Such a peaceful transition would not be the lot of Croatia where a non-communist government under Franjo Tudjman had been elected in 1990, a move prompted by the election of Serb nationalist Slobodan Milosević as Serbian Communist Party leader. Milosević harboured dreams of a 'Greater Serbia' and his rise to power within the powerful communist sector was seen by Croatia as a precursor of the implementation of a harsh communist rule over what remained of the Yugoslavian Republic under his presidency, with the result that Croatia declared its independence on 25 June 1991.

Fighting broke out immediately between Serbs living in the Krajina region of central and north-west Croatia, and Croatian forces and the Serbs declared the region as the

Republic of Serbian Krajina. The territorial loss was a damaging blow to the Croat nationalists, not only because of its strategic value but also to their recently declared but long-nurtured national pride.

In 1992 the United Nations succeeded in brokering a peace between the warring factions and deployed its United Nations Protection Force (UNPROFOR). Serb advances up to that time had taken 30 per cent of the former Yugoslav Republic of Croatia and the line was frozen by the UN, leaving many Croatians victims of Serbian ethnic cleansing in the Krajina region. The remaining 70 per cent of Croatia was recognised by the UN and the European Community as an independent state in January 1992.

In 1995, after nearly four years of smouldering resentment at the Serbian gains, Croatian forces launched an all-out offensive against the Serbs in Krajina, killing an estimated 14,000 Serbian civilians and creating more than 300,000 Serb refugees. Serb homes were burned, Serb property and businesses looted, and elderly Serbs dragged from their homes and shot where they stood. In retaliation, the Serbs launched a rocket attack on the Croatian capital of Zagreb, which caused a few deaths and injuries. But the most infamous of the spreading conflict was the war in Bosnia-Herzegovina where the sheer brutality and horrific campaigns of ethnic cleansing drew the attention of the world's media.

Bosnia had always been a multi-ethnic state with a considerable portion of the region shared by Serbs, Croats, and Bosnian Muslims known as Bosniaks. There were no clear geographical divisions between the groups and no one ethnic group held a clear majority. This meant that in order to create Slobodan Milosević dream of a 'Greater Serbia' – his favourite line was: 'Wherever there is a Serb, there is Serbia' – would mean the removal of all other ethnic groups in the area. As General Ratko Mladić would warn both Milosević and Radovan Karadžić co-founder of the Serbian Democratic Party and president of the Republika Srpska during the Srebrenica massacres: 'That is genocide'.

The Republika Srpska was created in 1992 with the aim of creating an ethnically pure Serbian enclave in northern and eastern Bosnia. The Croats meanwhile founded the Croatian Community of Herceg Bosna – Bosnia-Herzegovina – in much the same region. Fighting in the area occurred at first between Muslim forces and Bosnian Croat troops which were supported by the Croatian government in Zagreb. In 1994, Croatian forces were fighting in direct support of the Bosnian Croats until a ceasefire was agreed later that year with the foundation of the joint Federation of Bosnia-Herzegovina. The war with the Serbs continued and the new federation of Croats and Muslims now fought together against the Serbian forces.

Of these conflicts, the fighting between the Serbs and Bosnian Muslims was the most widely reported of the entire war and seemed to many European observers to be the whole crux of the conflict. The Serbs of Radovan Karadžić Republika Srpska, spurred on by Slobodan Milosević dream of a Greater Serbia, were set on the creation of a Serb homeland in an extended and ethnically pure Republika Srpska, but large Muslim minorities, especially in the cities, made it difficult for the Serbs to achieve their aim. As a result the Republika Srpska forces under General Ratko Mladić were committed to a policy of ethnic cleansing against Muslim communities on what the Serbian government considered as Serb lands. This included the reappearance of concentration camps in Europe, the first since World War II, rape and sexual assault against Muslim women and girls to 'breed out' the ethnic strain, and the mass executions of men and boys of military age.

The most infamous of these was the massacre in 1995 in the city of Srebrenica where, under the eyes of the Dutchbat UNPROFOR force, 7000 Muslims were killed by Serbian forces under the command of General Ratko Mladić It was a massacre of such immense proportions that the world paused to take breath. Srebrenica was a blood bath committed with such bestiality that its reverberations are felt across Europe today as a war crime that shocked the world.

In July 1995, soldiers of the Vojska Republika Srpska under the command of General Ratko Mladić also conducted the massacre of 30,000 refugees in the area of Srebrenica in Bosnia-Herzegovina. Eight thousand male Bosnians of all ages died in a campaign of ethnic cleansing more savage than that inflicted by the forces of Hitler's Third Reich on the Jewish population of Europe between 1933 and 1945. Also playing its part in the blood bath that shocked modern Europe was a feared Serbian paramilitary unit labelled The Skorpionis, named for its ability to strike rapidly and rid an area of its Muslim occupants, the hated Bosniaks, before forces of the United Nations, which had declared Srebrenica a UN-protected zone, could intervene. The Skorpionis operated as a paramilitary arm of the Serbian Interior Ministry until 1991.

Following the de facto dissolution of Yugoslavia in 1991 the Republic of Bosnia and Herzegovina declared its independence, sparking off a fierce struggle for territorial control within the republic among its three major ethnic groups. These were Bosnian Muslims known as Bosniaks, Bosnian Serbs, and Bosnian Croats. Of the three warring groups, the Croats tended to side with the Muslims, while the Serbs and Muslims engaged in a fierce war of attrition.

Srebrenica, located in Central Podrinje, was a strategically important region to the Serbs since it formed an integral part of their newly declared Republika Srpska. Possibly adhering to the well-worn maxim that a new broom sweeps clean, the Serbs decided the solution to the problem would be to eliminate the Bosniaks from their ethnic territories of Eastern Bosnia and Central Podrinje.

The ethnic cleansing of these areas, while not declared an official aim of the Bosnian Serbs at that time, began with attacks on Bosniak villages by paramilitary bands of local Serbs, resulting in the burning of Muslim homes and the slaughter of the Muslim population. Meanwhile, the Serbian Army prepared for its invasion of the territory and the capture of Srebrenica. The town fell to the Serbs in the early spring of 1992 and was recaptured by the Bosnian government forces a few months later.

Throughout 1992 the warring forces lost and regained territory. By Christmas of that year the Bosniak Army had fought through the divided territory to link up with Bosniak forces defending Žepa and Cerska, villages that would soon fall into the hands of the advancing Serbs as Mladić Serb Army advanced to capture the Muslim villages of Konjević Polje and to retake Cerska, effectively cutting the road to Žepa and reducing the size of the besieged region of Srebrenica and its environs to a mere 150 square kilometres. The Bosniak population fled east to Srebrenica and the population of the town almost doubled.

Siege conditions prevailed in Srebrenica as more and more Bosniak refugees sought shelter from the advancing Serbs.

The Serbs were determined to continue with their plan to take the town and cleanse the area of Muslims. On 13 April 1993 the Serb government told the UN High Commission for Refugees that it would attack the town within 48 hours unless the Muslim population surrendered and agreed to evacuation. Muslims in the town, by now having a good idea of what a Serbian-controlled 'evacuation' would entail, refused.

The Serb declaration, made in the face of the UN's declared state of Srebrenica as a safe area, prompted an emergency meeting of the United Nation's Security Council in New York to pass Resolution 819, which declared that: '*All parties and others concerned treat Srebrenica and its surroundings as a safe area which should be free from any armed attack or any hostile act*'. On 18 April the UN deployed its first batch of UNPROFOR troops to the region. The troops, and those that followed over the next 24 months, had a difficult task of keeping the two sides apart. Both Serb and Bosnian forces took advantage of the uneasy mandatory truce to launch attacks on each other. The Serbs blamed the UN. The Bosniaks blamed the UN. The penetration by the Serbs created a virtual blockade on the Dutch peacekeeping force. UN Dutch soldiers who went out of the enclave on leave were not allowed back in, reducing the number of standing UN forces within Srebrenica to less than 400. Food, medicine, equipment, and ammunition were also denied passage and within a few weeks the Dutch, under Dutchbat Commander Lieutenant-Colonel Thomas Karremans, were dangerously short of supplies. The resulting lack of materials made peacekeeping increasingly difficult for the Dutch, who were now having to contend with Bosnian forces which, aware of the Serb build-up, were using the UN-declared safe area as a base to launch attacks against the Serb Army.

In the spring of 1995 Radovan Karadžić the then president of the rogue Republika Srpska, ignored directives from the UN and ordered the Serb Army to penetrate deeply into the Srebrenica enclave. The mission task given to Serb commanders was to wipe out the Muslim population and gain as much territory as possible before the UN could force through its peace plan. The area was policed by a depleted UN Dutch peacekeeping force of 400 that now found itself overrun and threatened when the troops of Mladić closed in on the region and trapped the peacekeepers between opposing Serb and Bosnian forces.

By the summer of 1995 Bozniak civilians and military trapped within Srebrenica were dying of starvation. Sensing that the town's defences were demoralised, and with no sign of action from the international community, Serb president Karadžić ordered the forces of General Mladić to take the town. The vastly outnumbered Dutchbat UN troops either retreated into the town or surrendered as their observation posts came under fire. The defending Bosniak forces, low on men and ammunition, also retreated into the town. As a Swedish complex housing refugees was overrun by the Serbs, the 4000 Bozniak residents attempted to flee north into the town but many were cut down and massacred by the advancing Serbs. The UN peacekeeping force, outnumbered and trapped between the advancing Serbs and the Muslim defence perimeter, was powerless to help.

An incident which highlights the tenuous position of the Dutch was when a UN armoured vehicle attempted to withdraw after coming under fire from Serb tanks. An argument developed between the Dutch crew and the Bosniak defenders who insisted the UN vehicle remain in line. A hand grenade thrown by a Bosniak soldier exploded on the vehicle and killed a Dutchbat soldier. At the same time the Dutch were facing Serb heavy armour and their meagre force was harassed by Bosniak anti-tank fire from the rear.

By 10 July Serb forces of the Drina Corps were at the gates of the town and the Dutch UNPROFOR contingent, reluctant to engage in battle with such an obviously superior force, fired token warning shots over the heads of the advancing Serbs and withdrew behind the town's tottering defences. From there the Dutch commander sent urgent requests for NATO air support but throughout the day the skies above Srebrenica remained silent as NATO hovered on the brink of declaring full-out war on the Serbs. On 11 July, NATO rattled a feeble sabre when two Dutch F-16s, guided by the laser pointers of the British SAS, roared in to bomb Serb heavy armour as it advanced on the town, but the welcome, if frail, air support had to be cancelled due to poor visibility. In any event, a threat by Karadžić to order the execution of Dutch soldiers and French pilots captured by the Serbs led to a stand-down of the NATO air attacks.

With the town in the hands of the Serbs, Ratko Mladić

now turned his Drina Corps under its commander, General Živanović north towards the UN compound of Potocari where an estimated 30,000 Bosniak civilians had fled with the fall of Srebrenica. In the UN, frantic negotiations had broken out to secure the safety of the Muslim population in the Serb occupied territory but Radovan Karadžić had other plans. Along with presidential associate Momčilo Krajišnik he ordered Serb General Ratko Mladić to ensure that the region be 'swept clean' of the former Bosniak population, to which the general replied: 'People are not little stones, or keys in someone's pocket, that can be moved from one place to another, just like that... Therefore, we cannot precisely arrange for only Serbs to stay in one part of the country while removing others painlessly. I do not know how Mr Krajišnik or Mr Karadžić will explain that to the world. That is genocide.'

As Mladić received his orders and UN negotiations continued, the 30,000 civilians who had fled the Serb advance were now crowding into the UN compound at Potocari. Two thousand succeeded in gaining entry to the compound while others camped in neighbouring fields. The refugees were mainly made up of the elderly, women, and children, with a small minority of men, later estimated by the Dutch at around 1200. Food and water was at a premium and people among the crush of frightened refugees were dying of heat exhaustion as the fierce conditions took their toll.

By now the advancing Drina Corps had linked up with the main body of the Serbian Army and elements of the Skorpionis had surrounded the Potocari compound, clearing buildings of refugees and summarily executing the occupants. No discrimination was made between the old and the young, and babies barely out of the womb died with their skulls crushed against walls or under rifle butts. Old men and women were eviscerated by bayonets and young boys and girls submitted to multiple rapes before being despatched with a bullet to the head. The main target of men and youths of military age was forgotten among the carnage. Some refugees were seen to hang themselves or cut their own throats in terror of a more painful death at the hands of the rampaging Serbs.

Many reports would later circulate of the inaction of the Dutch peacekeepers to prevent the blood bath, one witness reporting the murder of a baby that was torn from its mother's arms and had its throat slit when a Serb objected to the infant's frenzied crying, this atrocity done under the eyes of Dutch soldiers who did nothing; but one would have had to be in the position of the Dutchbat soldiers to realise that they were a hair's breadth away from death themselves and that their lives depended on the whim of the blood-crazed Serb army.

On the morning of 12 July, agreement had been reached that buses would ferry the refugees north to Kladanj in Bosniak-held territory but as queues formed, Serb forces entered the Potocari compound and separated men and boys of military age into groups that were then marched away at rifle-point. The selection was purely arbitrary, with some elderly men and younger teenage boys ordered out of the line for the buses. The selected men and boys were taken to a holding point in Potocari where Dutchbat soldiers reported hearing occasional gunshots. A UN military observer who attempted to approach the holding area was turned back by Serb troops who made it clear he would be shot if he attempted to approach further.

The mass executions at Potocari were carried out blatantly in full view of the UNPROFOR contingent. At night, arc lights illuminated a scene reminiscent of the Nazi death camps as industrial bulldozers pushed the bodies of the dead and dying into mass graves. The rank smells of blood and putrefaction clung to the throats of those forced to witness the scenes and many of the Serb execution squads wore rags tied around their mouths and nostrils to avoid the stench of death. Streets were littered with corpses as the Serb forces continued with their rape and torture that had developed into a rage of ethnic hate. Noses, ears, and lips were cut from their victims as trophies, and parents were forced to watch their children murdered before their eyes. Many of the buses carrying women and children to Bosniak territory failed to reach their destination, the occupants ordered out of the vehicles en route and executed at the roadside.

It was clear that the Serbs were embarking on genocide on a massive scale, with reports that a column of 15,000 male refugees, who had attempted to break out of the Potocari perimeter to Tuzla on the night of 11 July, prior to the arrival of the Serbs, were ambushed by Serb artillery at Kemanica Hill between Konjević Polje and Nova Kasaba. Five thousand survivors of the shelling who had been at the rear of the column took to the woods alongside the road, where they hid from the Serb searchers.

Gradually, as thirst and hunger overcame them, the survivors of the artillery bombardment began to surrender or were captured by Serbs who promised their exchange for Serb PoWs. Some Serb soldiers were even reported to be wearing UN uniforms in an effort to get the Muslims to come out of hiding. The ruse worked and close to Sandići 300 surrendering Muslims were lined up in ranks before being mown down by machine-gun fire.

Only a few survived to tell their stories to the War Crimes Commission at The Hague. Among those killed were the political leaders of the Srebrenica enclave, medical staff of the local hospital at Potocari, and members of prominent Srebrenica families. Also killed were a number of women, children, and elderly who had chosen to accompany the column.

Reports of the Srebrenica massacres gradually filtered back to UN observers as the war continued through to the fall of 1995. At the end of August of that year NATO launched a bombing campaign that lasted until 20 September. NATO was aware of the criticism that its negotiations with the Bosnian Serbs had shown it to be weak and without conviction while thousands died, calling for the observation by one shrewd political observer that 'More might have been done if the Bosniaks' lifeline had been oil rather than beetroot soup...'. The war ended with the Dayton Peace Agreement of November 1995.

In the aftermath of the peace agreement the Dutch government accepted responsibility for the failure of the under-resourced Dutchbat mission to defend the population of Srebrenica and the cabinet resigned in 2002. A Serbian report issued in the same year and endorsed by leading Bosnian Serb politicians claimed that 1800 Muslim soldiers had died in combat, adding that '*the number of Muslim soldiers killed by Bosnian Serbs out of personal revenge or lack of knowledge of international law is probably around 100...*'

In 2004 a disputed Republika Srpska committee formed at the request of the international community's High Representative, Paddy Ashdown, released the names of 8731 persons confirmed missing or dead from the Srebrenica enclave. However, a resolution passed by the US House of Representatives a year later made it clear that the world saw the actions of the Serbs in Bosnia Herzegovina in 1995 *as genocide as defined in Article 2 of the Convention on the Prevention and Punishment of the Crime of genocide created in Paris on December 9 1948 and entered into force on January 12 1951'*.

By the fall of 2005, possibly demonstrating an anxiety to be accepted as part of the international community as well as that of the expanding EEC, the Special Bosnian Serb Government Working Group stated that 25,083 people were involved in the massacre at Srebrenica, including 19,471 members of Bosnian Serb armed forces that actively gave orders or directly took part in the massacre, claiming to have identified 17,074 by name. Eight hundred and ninety-two of those named still hold positions at, or are employed by, the government of the Republika Srpska. The names have not been revealed.

Up to 2006, 42 mass graves had been discovered around Srebrenica and 22 more are believed to exist in the area. The number of victims identified totalled 2070, with more than 7000 bags of body parts awaiting identification. At Kamenica Hill, site of the Artillery bombardment of a refugee column escaping from Potocari, another 1000 body parts were exhumed.

In May 2007 former Serb general Zdravko Tolimir was arrested by Serbian police and transferred to the International Criminal tribunal for the Former Yugoslavia in The Hague. Radovan Karadžić was arrested in Belgrade in July 2008. Former Serbian president Slobodan Milosević was accused of complicity in genocide in Srebrenica but died in March 2006 during his trial in The Hague before a verdict was returned.

Radovan Karadžić dubbed 'The Beast of Bosnia', was discovered working as a homeopathic doctor in Belgrade 13 years later. His face was almost covered by a long white bushy beard and side whiskers and his trademark bush of hair had been tamed into plaits. Karadžić went on trial at the War Crimes Tribunal in The Hague on charges of genocide in October 2009, refusing to recognise the authority of the court. The trial continued in his absence.

CHAPTER 5

THE CASE OF TWO LITTLE BECKHAMS

Soham, Cambridgeshire, England, 4 August 2002

'We're just off to buy some sweets'
— Jessica Chapman and Holly Wells,
on leaving the family barbecue.

August of 2002 in the heartland of Cambridgeshire was an unusually hot summer month. Families enjoyed leisurely strolls in the sunshine and children splashed in hurriedly purchased and erected plastic pools to cool off in the heat. In the town of Soham the families of best friends Holly Wells and Jessica Chapman were gathered for a barbecue in the back garden of the Wells family home in Red House Gardens. Amid the smells of grilled meat and wafting charcoal smoke the girls enjoyed the burgers and sausages and chatted about how they would spend the rest of the warm evening. They made an animated pair, both wearing their newly acquired red 'David Beckham' Manchester United strip with their heartthrob footballer's 'No 7' emblazoned on the back. Holly, who loved to dance and was a junior majorette with the local town band, was teaching her best friend some dance routines she had choreographed to tracks by her favourite group, S Club Juniors.

Just after 5.00 pm, Holly's mother Nicola Wells picked up her camera with the intention of taking photographs of the guests. Holly and Jessica, thoroughly excited by it all, begged to have a photograph taken of them together standing side-by-side below a wall clock in the Wells's hallway, their faces glowing from their recent exertions. Dark-haired Jessica wore an enigmatic half smile, her expression fixed and almost serious. Beside her, Holly grinned broadly, her long blonde hair parted in the middle and falling loosely on either side of her face, in contrast to Jessica's headband and beaded plait that ended in a colourful small tassel. The clock above their heads showed 5.04 pm.

The girls told their parents they intended to walk to the square at the war memorial some distance away to buy sweets and they set off hand-in-hand walking north along Sand Street. CCTV cameras would track their journey and show two pretty 10-year-old girls skipping happily together and laughing as they chatted, their bright red football shirts colourful as they caught the rays of the lowering summer sunlight. It was a sight that attracted the attention of a motorist driving with his wife along Sand Street. He would later recall to police how he pointed the girls out to his wife. 'Look,' he said, 'two little Beckhams.'

Like the parents of young girls everywhere, both the Wellses and Chapmans had made the girls aware of the potential dangers lurking beyond the safety of their homes and had imposed an 8.30 pm curfew that the girls had never broken. As 8.00 pm approached and the last of the Wellses' guests left, Nicola Wells telephoned the Chapmans, who had left an hour or so earlier. The news was worrying – the girls appeared to be missing. As 8.30 pm came and passed, both sets of parents became agitated and telephone calls between them became frequent. The late summer sunlight finally faded as a panicked Nicola Wells picked up the telephone to call the police. It was 10.00 pm.

Over the next few days it would be revealed that the girls had followed Sand Street to the war memorial but had found the sweet shop closed. Possibly recalling the vending machines in the nearby Ross Peers Sports Centre near their school, the girls had walked back down Gidney Lane to the Centre where a CCTV camera picked them up entering the foyer. There the trail vanished. It would later be deduced by investigators that the girls had probably decided to visit Maxine Carr, a 23-year-old former teaching assistant at St Andrews Primary School which the girls attended. Maxine Carr lived with her 28-year-old boyfriend, Ian Huntley, a caretaker at Soham Village College secondary school.

Carr's teaching contract at St Andrews had ended but she had remained a firm favourite with the girls, especially Holly, who had sent her a home-made leaving card with a large smiley face. The card read: 'It's class 12's special TA [teaching assistant], we will miss her a lot and will say, see you in the future Miss Carr, don't leave us, don't go far.' Fatefully, that weekend Maxine Carr was with her mother in Grimsby, while Ian Huntley was alone in the house that he and Carr rented at 5 College Close.

Huntley had just slammed the telephone down on Carr, whom he suspected of going out clubbing with her mother and associating with other men. He was very angry. Fate was about to take a dark turn for Holly and Jessica.

Huntley was divorced from his first wife when he and Carr met in a nightclub in Grimsby in February 2001. Huntley was 27 and Carr an immature 22, given to drinking heavily and flashing her breasts in public. Carr later moved in with Huntley to share his small flat in Barton-upon-Humber. At the time, Huntley was working as a barman and Carr soon found work in a fish-canning factory. To his associates Huntley was known as an emotional character given to fits of jealousy over Carr and subject to occasional bursts of anger. Huntley's father lived and worked as a school caretaker in the village of Littleport near Ely in Cambridgeshire and Huntley often drove down on his days off to help him at work. The relaxed nature of the work appealed to Huntley, so much so that he applied for the position of caretaker when it became available at Soham College, a mixed Comprehensive Foundation school for students aged 11–16. Had they lived, Holly and Jessica would have moved from St Andrews primary school in 2003 to study at the college, whose grounds adjoined those of the school.

Huntley's application was accepted, a bungled background check allowing a man who had previously been investigated as a suspect for sexual assaults to assume a position working within the proximity of children. His appointment would lead to an inquiry by the then Home Secretary, David Blunkett, into vetting methods for those working with children. Huntley began working at the college in November 2001 and Maxine Carr applied successfully for the temporary post of teaching assistant at St Andrews Primary, where she became very popular with the young students, especially Holly and Jessica.

The bodies of the two young girls would be found on 17 August by a gamekeeper who stumbled across their pathetic remains, half-burned and skeletonised, in an irrigation ditch 30 miles away from Soham near the perimeter fence of Lakenheath Royal Air Force base. By this time Ian Huntley was in custody but still vehemently denying any involvement in the girls' disappearance. Maxine Carr was also sticking to her story that she had been in the house with Huntley at the time the girls went missing, a lie she would later retract when evidence of Huntley's involvement became clear from DNA evidence found on the girls' bodies and in 5 College Close, the alleged murder scene.

Huntley had originally been trapped by a cut-off signal from Jessica Chapman's mobile phone which she was carrying at the time of her disappearance. By a sheer vagary of circumstance, unlike the majority of mobiles in the area Jessica's was connected to the Burwell Mast, which pinpointed the time that the phone was switched off as 18.46 BST. More tellingly, the location of the mobile at that time was either in or just outside 5 College Close.

Huntley had raised the suspicions of the police by his constant attendance at meetings convened to discuss the possible whereabouts of the missing girls. The school caretaker constantly badgered police and reporters for the latest developments of the case and joined in searches, even approaching Holly's father, Kevin Wells, and, in a cynical gesture that would not be defined until after his confession, passing on his condolences and sympathy to the bereft and grief-stricken father, telling him in a macabre double-entendre: 'I'm so sorry Kevin; I didn't know she was your daughter.' Both the Chapmans and Wellses, while not giving up all hope on the fate of their children, were beginning to accept the likelihood that Jessica and Holly were dead.

Following the discovery of the location of the signal from Jessica's mobile phone, Huntley became the investigators' prime suspect, and after the charred remains of Holly's and Jessica's shirts were found in a bin in a search of a building at Soham College – to which only Huntley held the key – he was arrested on suspicion and formerly charged with the girls' murders. Their bodies were discovered later the same day. Carr was arrested for assisting an offender in addition to conspiring to pervert the course of justice in her statement that placed her with Huntley on the evening of 4 November. Huntley was sectioned under the Mental Health Act and held at Rampton Hospital pending a hearing to establish if he was fit to stand trial. Despite his efforts to convince doctors that he was insane, Huntley *was* eventually found fit to stand trial.

Throughout lengthy interrogation both before and after the bodies were found, Ian Huntley had denied his involvement and he continued to claim his innocence, despite the weight of circumstantial evidence against him. The discovery at RAF Lakenheath had proved even more damning, since Huntley's father lived near to the airbase and Huntley often frequented the area around the perimeter on plane-spotting trips when visiting his father.

Just what had occurred in the house at 5 College Close after Huntley had lured the girls into entering – probably by lying that Maxine Carr was inside – will never be known, unless the killer speaks, but it seems without doubt that the motive was sexual. Decomposition and the burning of the corpses had made forensic examination to determine sexual abuse before death impossible but Huntley had had various near-miss brushes with the law over alleged rapes and sexual assaults, as well as burglary. Oddly these cases never reached the ears of those who vetted him for the position of caretaker at Soham Village College, even though the previous holder of the position had left after it was discovered that he had maintained an improper relationship with a girl pupil. These were questions that would be raised after the trial and the result would be the introduction of a law that required any adult working in the proximity of children to be licensed, at their own cost, to do so.

The case went to trial at London's Old Bailey on 5 November 2003, with Huntley represented by Stephen Coward, a seasoned 'silk' who had defended at many murder and fraud trials. The prosecution opened its case by accusing Huntley of murder and Carr of attempting to pervert the course of justice. It was alleged that Huntley had made Carr aware of his part in the girls' disappearance on her return from Grimsby and together they had concocted the alibi that she was in the house with Huntley and had seen the girls leave alive.

The thunderbolt came when prosecution counsel, Richard Latham QC, revealed that the prosecution understood from the defence that it was 'unlikely to be disputed' by Huntley that the two girls went into his house shortly after 6.30 pm that evening; that Huntley was the only person there at the time; that the girls died within a short time of going inside his home; and that it was Huntley who took their bodies to the place where they were found.

The admission by Huntley that he was alone with the girls contradicted Maxine Carr's statement that she was with Huntley that evening, which she would later excuse as her concern that he would be 'fitted up' for a crime he didn't commit on the basis of a past rape inquiry in which he had been a suspect and later acquitted. Huntley's admission appeared likely to be construed as an admission of murder but none, other than his defence counsel and Huntley himself, were prepared for the story he was to tell from the witness box when he took the stand the next day.

According to Huntley, Holly and Jessica had arrived looking for Maxine at around 6.30 pm, just as he had finished bathing his dog, Sheba. He told them Carr was away and invited them into the house, where Holly developed a nosebleed in the bedroom, with a few drops of blood staining the sheet, which she apologised for. He then took her into the bathroom to clean up and she sat on the edge of the bath which was half-full from the dog-washing episode. Huntley then maintained that as he reached across Holly to wet some toilet tissue under the bath tap he accidentally knocked her into the bath, whereupon Jessica began screaming that he had deliberately pushed her friend.

Huntley's tale reached the bounds of fantasy when he

then told the court he had lifted the unconscious Holly from the bath and laid her on the carpet in the bedroom, where he detected signs of life. He then left Holly to take the hysterical Jessica downstairs to the lounge to explain it had all been an accident, when Jessica attempted to make a call on her mobile phone. He snatched the phone and switched it off, at which point she attempted to open the front door. He pulled her back with a hand across her mouth and another at her throat when, according to Huntley, she expired.

The media couldn't believe its luck. Huntley's story was so fantastic that no one other than his counsel could profess to believe any part of it. It was very unlikely that the girls, both intelligent and aware of the dangers, would have gone into the house if they had known Huntley was there on his own. In the bathroom, why did Huntley reach around Holly to access the bath tap when there was a hand-basin at his elbow, and why did he not attempt to revive the 'unconscious' and half-drowned Holly? The reaction of a person falling backwards into a bath full of water, even the six-inch level estimated by investigators, is to throw their arms wide and clutch for support. It is extremely unlikely that they would fall with such force, their fall cushioned by the water, to knock them unconscious enough to inhale sufficient water to drown in seconds. A person would have to be struck with extreme force to bring about unconsciousness and investigators had noticed a large crack in the side of the acrylic bath.

Again, Huntley insisted that Holly was alive when he pulled her from the bath, yet he admitted to making no attempt to revive her, instead leaving her alone on the bedroom carpet while he went downstairs with the other girl. It was more than likely to the prosecution – and possibly at this stage to the defence – that Huntley had in all probability attempted to sexually abuse one or both of the girls in the heat of lust and then killed them to ensure their silence.

On the Monday morning after the disappearance he had been seen by neighbours washing his Ford Fiesta car and ripping out the boot floor covering which he replaced with domestic carpeting. Huntley would admit years later that he had hidden the girls' bodies in his car boot over the weekend and driven them to Lakenheath where he dumped the corpses in the irrigation ditch after cutting off their clothing with scissors. He returned with the clothing to Soham College and burned it in a metal rubbish bin where the charred remains were later discovered in a police search. He later returned to the spot where he had dumped the bodies to pour gasoline over the remains and set them alight in an effort to destroy any DNA evidence.

Huntley had also shown his calculating nature, far removed from a panicked individual who has seen two young people die accidentally, by driving his car to a garage in Ely, some miles away, to have the barely worn tyres replaced, clearly as a precaution in case police checked tyre tracks at Lakenheath, even paying the fitter a bribe of £10 to enter a false car registration number on the receipt. None of Huntley's actions were those of an innocent man trapped in a web of circumstances, and he was found guilty of two counts of murder and sentenced to two life sentences after a five-week trial.

Maxine Carr, who was tried concurrently with Huntley, was sentenced to serve three-and-a-half years for attempting to pervert the course of justice and giving aid to a felon. She was released after serving half of her sentence and given a new identity. An order was passed by the High Court in February 2005 protecting her new identity indefinitely.

Huntley went on to attempt suicide, leaving a tape that further involved Carr in covering up the killing of the two girls. He will be due for release in 2042.

CHAPTER 6

THE FRITZL ABDUCTION

Amstetten, Austria, 1984–2008

'My daughter has joined a cult'
> – Joseph Fritzl explaining his daughter's
> disappearance in 1984.

In *The Descent of Man* Charles Darwin acknowledged that 'of all the differences between man and the lower animals, the moral sense or conscience is by far the most important'. He was particularly interested in whether natural selection had played its part in shaping a natural aversion to incest among human beings, possibly because the offspring of liaisons outside the tribe and family tended to survive in larger numbers. Certainly, in the case of humankind Nature has left her own trap for the incestuous. In the 21st century, biologists are aware that DNA is formed of 46 chromosomes, half of which is equally contributed by the biological father and mother. Should one of those 23 chromosomes supplied by each partner prove faulty, an inbuilt 'fail-safe' provides that it is naturally backed up by the corresponding healthy chromosome supplied by the other sexual partner. In incestuous relationships the chance of two corresponding chromosomes being faulty is heightened and the abnormalities of inbreeding result.

So what therefore causes a father to lust after his daughter to such an extent that he will remove her from society to be his personal sex slave and hide her in a location unknown to all but himself? The disclosure of what was discovered in Austria in 2008 shook the world for its sheer bestiality, and for its incredibility. This was behaviour far beyond the mores of humanity. These were the actions of a monster.

In April 2008, a pale-faced, grey-haired woman entered the police station in the picturesque town of Amstetten in Lower Austria and told detectives a strange tale. Her name was Elisabeth Fritzl and she claimed that for 24 of her 42 years she had been imprisoned underground by her father, Josef. While in captivity she had borne him eight children, one of whom was stillborn. She said that her eldest daughter Kerstin and her sons Stefan and Felix had shared her captivity all their lives. Kerstin was 19 years old, Stefan 18, and Felix five.

Three other children, Lisa, Monika, and Alexander, had been brought up by her father and his wife Rosemarie above ground, Josef Fritzl having pretended that they were foundlings left on her parents' doorstep by Elizabeth whom, he told associates, had run away from home aged 18 (on the day he had locked her away in her underground prison). The detectives heard there was a seventh child who had lived only three days before dying of a respiratory complication. It would transpire that Fritzl had disposed of the body in the cellar furnace.

Josef Fritzl was a native of Amstetten, born in the town in April 1935, three years before Austria was annexed to Nazi Germany by Hitler and four years before the start of World War II. He and Rosemarie were married in 1957 when she was 17 and together they produced seven children. Elisabeth was born in 1966 and as she grew to womanhood her pale, ethereal beauty attracted her dominant father who, she later revealed, began to sexually abuse her when she was 11 years old. That abuse, which included all kinds of sexual perversions, usually occurred on solitary walks together, car trips, or visits to the cellar when Fritzl insisted that the young Elisabeth help him in his underground workshop. All this occurred without the knowledge of Rosemarie Fritzl, who appears to have been a frail and timid wife, bullied by her husband and careful not to offend him with any questions that may have plagued her mind.

As is usual in the case of abused children, Elisabeth became withdrawn and sullen as she reached early womanhood and became known among her school friends for her rebellious nature, openly disobeying teachers' instructions, to the amusement of her classmates. After leaving school at 15 she started a catering course to train as a waitress. Two years later she ran away from home with a work friend and the two girls went into hiding in Vienna, working as waitresses in the capital's bijou tea bars to earn their living.

Elisabeth's freedom from the abuse of her father lasted for just three weeks when the girls were found by police after being reported missing, and returned to their parents. Cowed by her father, Elisabeth was once again forced to submit to his perversions as the obsessed Fritzl sought to dominate his daughter even more. Fritzl's warped mind had now converted his daughter into the role of his concubine and his fear of losing control of her came to a head in the summer of 1984 when, having now completed her interrupted training in catering, Elisabeth was offered a job in nearby Linz.

Josef Fritzl commenced with his horrific plan to keep Elisabeth for his own perversions by starting to excavate the cellar under the house. The house was large, with more than 66 rooms, many of which Fritzl let out to tenants, and the cellar extended some distance out under the rear garden. By removing earth from between the foundations of an older demolished building that had once occupied land behind the house, Fritzl was able to construct a series of tunnels that linked five small rooms. These were accessed from behind a sliding storage shelf off Fritzl's small workshop which gave on to a narrow door. This led into a soundproofed enclosure from which the underground living accommodation began, concealed and guarded by a heavy steel door. Beyond this, Fritzl had constructed a storage room for provisions and a washing machine, beyond that a narrow passage led to a sleeping area measuring 3 x 3 metres. Another narrow passage led to a living area, again just three metres square, into which was crammed a washing area, toilet, and kitchenette. A 60-centimetre-wide passage along which an adult would have to turn sideways to gain comfortable movement, led into the final room, again hewed out of the foundations to form a cramped three-metre-square area that contained a double bed and a TV.

The day Fritzl chose to strike was 29 August. He told Elisabeth that he needed help in carrying a door down to his workshop. Elisabeth was accustomed to such summonses and knew what they usually entailed, so mentally prepared herself for the inevitable paternal rape and accompanied her father below ground. There he led her through the hidden sliding door and Elisabeth must have wondered why her father should have use for such concealment. Certainly, when arriving at the heavy steel door that her father expected her to hold in place while he fitted the extra-strong hinges she must have questioned why he hadn't called on one of his sons for help with such heavy work.

Nonetheless, Elisabeth struggled with her task and finally the door was hanging in its place. Then she felt rough towelling wrapped around her mouth, soaked in a liquid that she couldn't identify but which made her head swim and her legs buckle. Elisabeth passed into unconsciousness as her father pressed the ether-soaked cloth against her mouth and nostrils. At that moment she passed from freedom to a claustrophobic captivity that was to rob her of her youth and keep her slave to an incestuous monster for the next 24 years.

Elisabeth recovered consciousness to find herself in strange, dark surroundings handcuffed to a metal pole. The air she breathed was moist and earthy and there was total darkness. At first the petrified young woman thought she was dead and wept with fear. She called out but her voice seemed to be swallowed by the walls, just the faint echo of a tomb. Her horror lasted for weeks, chained in misery with the handcuffs removed only when her father returned to rape her in return for bringing her food. Elisabeth acquiesced to his repulsive advances because, as she was to tell police 24 years later, it was a choice between rape or starvation.

A week after her daughter's disappearance Elisabeth's mother Rosemarie informed the police. A month later Fritzl gave police a letter from Elisabeth postmarked in Brannau, a town some distance away. In it, Elisabeth had been forced to write that she was with a friend and did not wish to return to her family. At first there appeared to be no cause for alarm, as the rebellious Elisabeth had run away from home twice in the past and had been discovered living with friends both times and brought back to her parents by police. Now she was 18 and legally allowed to live where she chose.

Her 18th birthday had obviously played a part in Fritzl's master plan. Later, letters would arrive regularly purportedly from Elisabeth telling her parents that she was now living with a cult and not to worry as she was well. Throughout the years of Elisabeth's captivity Fritzl continued to force his captive to write letters about her new life and he even once impersonated his daughter during a telephone conversation with his wife. That deceit occurred in 1993 when Elisabeth was nine years into her captivity and a mother of four children, now pregnant with Monika, her fifth.

Fritzl's plan was to gradually introduce his incestuous brood to his wife by pretending that Elisabeth was leaving children on her parents' doorstep with pleas to look after them. The child left on this occasion was nine-month-old Lisa, who would be followed in succession by Monika and Alexander. The couple adopted Lisa and became foster carers for the second and third child. All was overseen by the local social services who fell for Fritzl's apparently, to them, plausible explanation of the babies' mysterious appearance on his doorstep.

In 2003 Elisabeth gave birth to twin boys, Felix and Michael, but here nature caught up with the incestuous Fritzl. Michael was born a weak child with a respiratory condition not uncommon among premature babies in which the unformed lungs are unable to hold air. Within three days the child died and Fritzl callously burned the body in the solid fuel stove that provided heat for the underground rooms. The other twin, Felix, survived and would continue to live underground with his mother, elder sister Kerstin and brother Stefan – all of them stooped due to the 1.60 metre head-height of the low ceilings, and with a crippled gait caused by lack of exercise.

Despite their physical disabilities, Elisabeth's indomitable spirit meant that her children learned to read and write under her tutelage. The children also accepted Fritzl as their grandfather, the father of their mother as well as their own. In other words, their view of human interaction and society was tribal. Even their language was personal to 'the tribe', communicating with their mother by hisses and grunts while speaking normally in their grandfather's presence, which occurred at least three times a week when he brought food that he purchased in outlying towns and supermarkets and smuggled into the cellar at night. On occasions, what Fritzl judged as bad behaviour would be punished by the lights in the basement being switched off and no food delivered for several days at a time.

On 19 April 2008, Elisabeth's eldest daughter, Kerstin, collapsed from kidney failure brought on by the enforced lifestyle underground, and Elisabeth pleaded with her captor to allow the girl hospital treatment. Fritzl, who would later tell investigators that he had. a scheme to introduce Elisabeth and her children back into society later that year, finally agreed and Elisabeth helped carry her daughter above ground, tasting the air of the outside world for the first time in 24 years. She then dutifully returned to the underground prison to be with her children while she awaited news of Kerstin's condition.

Fritzl would later admit that he had grown tired of the subterfuge involved in maintaining his hidden family. At 73 his sexual urges had waned and he no longer found 42-year-old Elisabeth attractive: a cold statement from a monster who had reduced a pretty young girl to a wizened crone by keeping her locked underground for 24 years.

Above ground, Kerstin was rushed to the Landesklinikum Amstetten and immediately placed in the intensive care unit. Later that day Fritzl appeared at the hospital with a note he claimed was written by the girl's mother, giving him authority to discuss Kerstin's case with doctors. This time his charm failed to work on medical staff and they informed police of their concerns two days after Kerstin was admitted. An appeal was made by police for Kerstin's mysterious mother to come forward. Fritzl, caught in his own web of deceit, finally admitted that Kerstin's mother was his 'runaway' daughter Elisabeth and produced a letter allegedly written four months earlier and posted in the town of Kematen. Elisabeth, he insisted, was still in the clutches of a cult.

Now suspicious of the 'worried' grandfather, police

checked Fritzl's background and found that the guesthouse proprietor had a criminal record. It transpired he had been arrested twice on suspicion of arson, twice for sex offences and had served a prison sentence for raping a woman at knifepoint. The reason that his record hadn't emerged when he applied to adopt the baby Lisa was that Austrian law existing at the time of his application ruled that sex offences were removed from the record after 10 to 15 years depending on their severity.

The police then contacted cult specialist Manfred Wohlfahrt who expressed doubt at the existence of a cult. Austria is a comparatively small country and Wohlfahrt knew of no local cult where Elisabeth could be hiding. He also criticised the letters produced by Fritzl, finding them stilted, as if they had been written to dictation from another person. Elisabeth would have seen some of these issues reported and debated on television as she sat underground, still barred from the outside world.

Any thought of escape from her dungeon was tempered by threats from Fritzl that the outer metal door was connected to a voltage high enough to kill anyone who tampered with the lock from inside. On the exterior, the door had a keypad lock, the combination of which was known to Fritzl alone. This leads one to speculate on the state of mind of a man who saw no danger in taking holidays abroad with friends during Elisabeth's incarceration, yet should he suffer an accident or a heart attack it would have left her and her children condemned to a horrendous slow death from starvation. Many see Fritzl as a cold and calculating monster. Others believe he was totally insane.

Elisabeth's tearful pleas to be allowed to visit her sick daughter forced her father to move forward his plans to introduce his 'satellite family' to society. On 26 April his wife Rosemarie was startled by the appearance of a daughter she had not seen for 24 years followed by a teenager and a child who she was told were her grandchildren. Fritzl introduced them to his wife with the story that he had finally tracked down the cult which had held his daughter and grandchildren and rescued them. Rosemarie must have had her doubts, since a telephone call back in 1993 in which Fritzl had impersonated his daughter had been made only two days after the Fritzl's telephone number had been changed. How would Elisabeth have known the new number? But like dominated wives everywhere, Rosemarie Fritzl hadn't dared to question her husband on the slightest fault. Although she would be arrested on suspicion of complicity later, police were soon convinced that this simple homely woman had known nothing of what was occurring beneath her home for more than two decades.

On the day of her release from the cellar, Elisabeth and Fritzl went to the hospital to visit Kerstin. The previously primed staff telephoned the police to inform them that the mother and grandfather were present and they were both detained for questioning and taken to the police station. There, Elisabeth refused to tell her story until she was assured that she and her children would be protected from Fritzl. Meanwhile, in another interrogation room Fritzl continued with the story of his heroic rescue of Elisabeth from the religious cult that had held her captive. His protestations were in vain. For two hours detectives had listened aghast to Elisabeth's story of imprisonment and incestuous rape. Fritzl was arrested on charges of serious crimes against family members, including false imprisonment, kidnap, rape, manslaughter by negligence and incest. That night, as he sat in a prison cell awaiting his fate, Elisabeth, her children, and her mother Rosemarie were taken into care.

A few days later Fritzl broke and confessed to imprisoning his daughter and of having fathered seven children. Police who examined the underground dungeon were horrified at the conditions the young woman and her children had had to endure. The stench of body sweat and cooking residues and the high levels of CO_2 must have made life intolerable. The crude air venting system that Fritzl had installed back in 1984 was hardly sufficient to support one individual, let alone a family.

Fritzl was arraigned to go to trial in St Pölten on 15 March 2009. Although his defence questioned the charges of unlawful imprisonment and rape – both of which Frtizl now maintained was consensual – after a trial lasting four days he was found guilty of the murder by negligence of the infant, Michael, as well as the enslavement, rape, incest, coercion, and false imprisonment of his daughter Elisabeth. He was sentenced to life imprisonment.

Josef Fritzl is now rumoured to be writing a book in his cell, in which he describes his formative years growing up under a Nazi regime. The 73-year-old depraved monster is kept in solitary confinement, following death threats from other prisoners. Elisabeth and her children are undergoing a lengthy programme of rehabilitation to introduce them to a world that the children had never known. In their years of enforced imprisonment with their mother, Stefan and

Felix had never seen snow, a tree, or a motor car – except on the second-hand television set provided by Fritzl. Although taught to read and write by their mother, the boys still communicate in their own language of coos and grunts. All, including their grandmother, Rosemarie, are under regular psychiatric treatment that is expected to last for many years. All are victims of the monster known to the world as Josef Fritzl, whom fellow prisoners call Satan.

CHAPTER 7

THE LARGEST ART ROBBERY IN EUROPE

Zurich, Switzerland, 10 February 2008

'They knew exactly what they were looking for'
— A museum guard after the robbery.

It was the artist Augustus John who said a portrait is a painting in which the mouth isn't quite right, but despite the vagaries of the old masters, their paintings are still much sought after by collectors — the genuine and the unscrupulous. The theft of art — be it sculptures, precious antiques, or paintings by old or modern masters — ranks high on the world's list of the most profitable criminal enterprises, third only behind drugs and arms sales. The Art Market Research Index, which monitors 50 per cent of the world's listed art, shows that rising art prices, and the particular psychology of art collecting, has seen prices for modern art rise three times since 2002. While it holds true that the investment market in impressionist and modern art has slumped due to the current world economic crisis, the trade in old masters paintings, when and if they come onto the market, is still volatile.

Such is the desire to own a Cézanne, Degas, or Van Gogh that some of the more unscrupulous collectors will pay a king's ransom to possess a masterpiece kept in a private vault for their individual pleasure and viewing. The Zurich art robbery of 2008 may well have been planned and executed with such high prices in mind.

On Sunday, 10 February 2008, three armed and masked men carried out the most audacious art theft in world history when they raided the privately owned Emil Bührle Art Museum in Zurich, Switzerland, and stole four eighteenth-century paintings by old masters artists Degas, Cézanne, Van Gogh, and Monet, to the staggering value of US$163.2 million. The robbery took place in broad daylight just as the museum was preparing to close its doors to visitors.

The museum is located in the Bührle villa, a large house in a normally quiet, residential street in the upmarket Seefeld area of Zurich. Half an hour before the museum was due to close, a white Opel saloon approached the building at high speed and slewed to a stop before the doors amid a cloud of gravel and dust, leaving museum attendants frozen in their actions and gaping at the three men wearing ski masks and brandishing handguns who burst from the vehicle. The men rushed into the museum and two of the robbers, obviously well briefed and familiar with the building's layout, raced up to the first floor and made immediately for the exhibition hall. There they threatened staff and visitors before removing four paintings from the walls – Cézanne's 'Boy in a Red

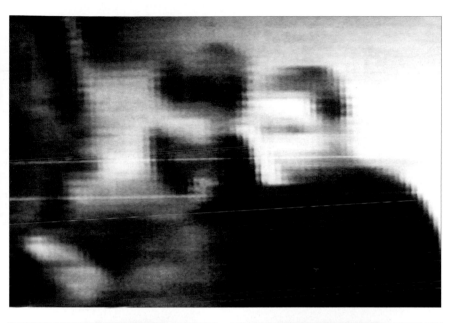

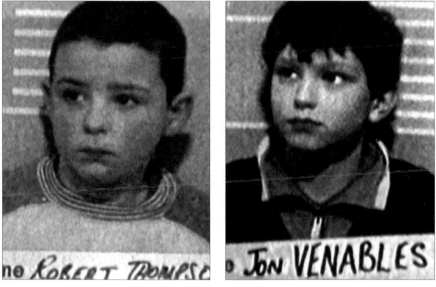

Above: Looking through the security tapes from the shopping centre where James Bulger disappeared, Police were eager to trace these two young boys.

Below: They were two ten-year-olds, Robert Thompson (*left*) and Jon Venables (*right*), who were later convicted of James' murder.

Above: Fledgling model Sally Ann Bowman (*left*) was murdered in the driveway of her home in Croydon, south London (*right*) in 2005.

Below: The belongings of the victims of the Srebrenica massacre, the largest mass murder in Europe since the Second World War, lie strewn by the side of the road, July 1995.

Holly Wells (*left*) and Jessica Chapman (*right*) in their prized Manchester United shirts, photographed on that dreadful day in August, 2002 when they were murdered by Ian Huntley.

Above: The house in Amstetten, Austria, that served as both a home and a prison to members of the Fritzl family.

Below: A photograph of Elizabeth (*left*), taken before she was lured into the basement by her own father, Josef Fritzl (*right*). She was held prisoner and abused by him for 24 years.

Above: The Zurich museum that was the scene of a daring armed robbery in February 2008. The thieves took four paintings – by Monet, Degas, Van Gogh and Cezanne – that had a combined estimated value of £85million.

Below: Donald Neilson, the 'Black Panther', is pictured leaving the Newcastle court in 1978. He abducted and murdered 17-year-old Leslie Whittle in 1975.

Above: Three-year-old Madeleine McCann disappeared while on holiday with her parents in Praia da Luz, Portugal, in May 2006. Her whereabouts remain a mystery.

Below: Madeleine's parents, Kate and Gerry McCann, pictured just two days after the disappearance of their daughter. Kate is holding Madeleine's favourite toy, her pink 'Cuddle Cat'.

Above: One of the photographs that was sent by Virginia Tech University Killer Seung-Hui Cho to the American News Channel NBC. He killed 32 people and wounded many others before killing himself.

Below: The body of Douglas Wainwright – one of Michael Ryan's 16 victims – is slumped at the wheel of his Datsun Bluebird, covered with a blanket. The Hungerford massacre of 1987 led to a tightening of the laws on the ownership of firearms in the UK.

Above: Eric Harris (18) and Dylan Klebold (17) are caught on CCTV during the murderous rampage at their school in Columbine in April 1999.

Below: Columbine student Loren Moulton is reunited with her mother after the shootings.

Waistcoat', Degas's 'Viscount Lepic and his Daughters', Monet's 'Poppies Near Véthueil', and Van Gogh's 'Blooming Chestnut Branches'.

Downstairs, meanwhile, the third gunman threatened the stunned museum staff with a handgun and made them all lie face down on the floor. Within minutes the paintings were taken outside and placed in the boot of the car which promptly sped off in the same manner as its arrival with the three robbers on board. The shocked staff were unsure whether the car was driven by a fourth man or by one of the three robbers. One shaken attendant later reported to police: 'We were ordered to the floor by a man who spoke German with a Slavic accent. Then there was a clatter of feet and they were gone. It was all so fast we didn't have time to think...'

All the works were in the collection amassed by Emil Bührle, a German munitions magnate who had taken over the Oerlikon arms factory near Zurich in the late 1920s. Bührle became a naturalised Swiss citizen in 1936 and retained contacts among the rising Nazi hierarchy through his armament contracts in World War II. Having studied art history in Germany in his youth, Bührle was ideally placed to track down art looted from the Jews and spent some time in Paris in the war years seeking out art for another avid collector, Nazi Foreign Minister Joachim von Ribbentrop. The Bührle Collection is viewed as controversial because Emil Georg Bührle was a major supplier of arms to the Allied and Axis powers during World War II. The collection is also believed to contain several art works looted or bought cheaply from European Jews fleeing Nazi persecution in the late 1930s.

But despite the export of Oerlikon armaments to Nazi Germany, when between 1940 and 1945 Oerlikon accounted for 52 per cent of arms exports from Switzerland, as a Swiss naturalised citizen operating a Swiss-based company Bührle escaped the fate of Alfried Krupp in 1945 and indulged himself in creating his immensely valuable collection of art, mainly purchased from 1951 up to his death in 1956.

The Bührle robbery, apart from being Europe's biggest art theft, attracted the attention of the world media especially because it followed the theft of two Pablo Picasso oil paintings from a cultural exhibition in eastern Switzerland four days earlier, where they had featured as exhibits on loan from the Sprengel Museum in Germany.

As is customary in art thefts, the paintings were immediately listed as missing in the Art Loss Register, which would make them immensely difficult to sell through a small dealer or auction house, therefore the Swiss police assumed they had been stolen to order by one or various collectors. To be fair, this theory was marred by the fact that the paintings had been hanging in a line in the order they were taken, so the choice may have been dictated only by the circumstances, although the most valuable of those stolen, the Cézanne, would fetch a very high price running into many millions even if sold clandestinely.

Certainly, some specialists involved in tracking down stolen art doubted that the gang, while obviously very professional and well organised, had a buyer in their sights, especially when two of the paintings showed up abandoned in a parked car some days after the robbery.

They also pointed out that removing a bulky, mounted painting was outside the usual manner of art thieves – the Cézanne and Monet alone measured over 80 centimetres by 65 centimetres each and would have been awkward to disguise or carry. Most stolen paintings are removed from the frame with a sharp knife, as in the case of the infamous Mona Lisa theft from the Louvre in 1911. The paintings stolen did not make up the most valuable bundle in the museum's collection and the mix of value and quality adds to the impression that the robbery was as haphazard as it was brazen.

A reward of 100,000 Swiss francs was immediately offered for information leading to the recovery of the paintings. Leading the hunt was Chief Inspector Rueeger of the Zurich police, who announced the possibility that the theft was connected to the earlier Picasso thefts. The tenuous connection was the fact that a white car had been involved in both crimes.

The discovery of a white Opel Omega in a car park outside Zurich University's psychiatric clinic a week later gave weight to the theory when a search revealed two of the missing paintings on the rear seat. The museum, and no doubt its insurers, rejoiced at the return of Van Gogh's 'Blossoming Chestnut Branches' and Monet's 'Poppies Near Vétheuil', but the hunt for the Cézanne and Degas would have to continue. Amid rumours that a ransom had been paid for the return of the two recovered paintings, which were valued jointly at around US$70 million, Zurich police commandant Phillip Hotzenkeocherie ordered more men into the hunt. Meanwhile, the relieved insurers debated how much of the advertised 100,000 Swiss francs would be paid to the dazed 56-year-old parking attendant who had spied the paintings in the car on a routine patrol.

While Bührle Museum curator Lukas Gloor was roused from his gloom by the return of two of the stolen paintings, the more valuable Cézanne and Monet remain lost somewhere in the murky world of clandestine art collecting. Estimates vary widely for such rare and rarely sold works – the Cézanne alone is valued at US$90 million in some circles, meaning that the auction sale value of the haul is far greater than the US$163.5 million proposed for insurance purposes. At the time of writing, the fates of the stolen Cézanne and Monet are not known. Like the Van Gogh and the Degas stolen with them, they may well have been abandoned but, unlike the recovered paintings, left in a place where they will not come to light for many years. They may equally have been destroyed because their fame and the notoriety of the robbery combined to make them un-sellable.

The largest art robbery in the world is generally accepted to be the one that took place in 1990 at the Isabella Stewart Gardner Museum in Boston, USA, when works stolen were estimated in value at US$300 million, according to the Federal Bureau of Investigation's art theft website.

CHAPTER 8

LITTLE GIRL LOST

Praia da Luz, Portugal, 3 May 2007

'This has been the bestest day of all'
    — Madeleine McCann, discussing the holiday with
        her mother on the day she disappeared.

One of the most baffling mysteries that stunned the world in recent years occurred on the Portuguese Algarve coast in 2007. Nearly three years later the mystery remains and everyone has an opinion on what happened and who was to blame. But still, no guilt has been asserted and no one charged. Yet there is no doubt that a crime was committed, since it involved the disappearance of a female child from a holiday apartment, just a few days before her fourth birthday.

At the time of her disappearance the girl was alone except for her younger twin siblings. Their parents were dining with friends at a nearby restaurant. Neighbours in the apartment block heard nothing until the anguished mother's screams erupted as she discovered that her daughter was missing.

The missing child was Madeleine McCann. Her parents, medical doctors Gerry and Kate McCann, later admitted leaving their children alone in apartment 5A of the Mark Warner Ocean Club complex of Praia da Luz on 3 May 2007 while they spent the evening with friends who had travelled with them in the same holiday group. Police called to the scene found the front door of the apartment that gave onto the upper car park ajar. The metal roller shutter that normally shielded the window of the children's bedroom was open sufficiently to have provided access for an intruder to the sleeping children. Madeleine's brother and sister, 16-month-old Sean and Amelie, had slept in twin cots placed in the middle of the room. Madeleine's bed, from which it was first assumed she had been taken, was against the wall furthest from the window.

In those first shocked moments when the realisation dawned that Madeleine was gone from apartment 5A, there was a frenzied search of the small gardens, hardly more than paved enclosures, at the rear of blocks 4 and 5, and the upper car-parking area fronting the apartment blocks. The streets around the Waterside Garden complex of Praia da Luz were well lit at night but every urban development has its shadows.

With the knowledge that the rear patio door had been left ajar, initially there seemed to be no doubt that Madeleine had walked out of the apartment through the unlocked rear patio doors. Unfortunately this fact was not available to investigators until later. No one, however, except it seemed the child's parents, could contemplate the horror of abduction. Madeleine was just a little girl. Who would take her and why?

The officer in charge of the hunt was Detective Chief Inspector Gonçalo Amaral, a heavyweight in the police force at nearby town of Portimão. DCI Amaral was an investigator renowned for never giving up on a case. He was also a man of fixed opinions who proved to be unshakeable once he convinced himself of the assumed facts. Certain aspects of the crime scene in apartment 5A of Waterside Gardens did not ring true to his policeman's intuition.

The discovery of Madeleine McCann's disappearance had led to a gathering of local police and concerned well-wishers. The area outside the bedroom window bore the imprints of many shoes as neighbours (and many others) had sought to view and even photograph the window sill across which the child appeared to have been abducted — except that she wasn't. Along with any resident who had lost his or her door key to a dwelling whose windows or patio doors are protected by the *persianas metálicas* in use at the apartment blocks in Waterside Gardens, Amaral and his colleagues knew that the shutters offered no access and that any attempt to force them upwards would cause the links to lock in the interior roller box. Moreover, no marks were present on the window's mossy sill which might provide evidence of an attempt to force the shutter. In short, whoever took Madeleine had other access to the seemingly locked apartment.

Because of this, DCI Amaral immediately suspected the child's parents of complicity in her disappearance, and thus began the nightmare of Gerry and Kate McCann. After all, if no one had broken into the apartment through the shutters, how had the child disappeared from inside? Unfortunately, the chief detective's suspicions — in the absence of his knowledge of the unlocked patio door – were sufficient to close down any reasonable avenue of search for the missing child and much valuable time was lost as he moved the investigation in a direction dictated by his suspicions that Gerry and Kate McCann had killed their own daughter and disposed of the body before calling the police. He was later to publish a book, *Maddie – a Verdad da Mentira,* based on his own conclusions of the case, of which the McCanns' lawyers successfully obtained a High Court ban on publication.

Amaral's suspicions were reasonably based on the fact that someone had opened the metal bedroom shutter and the front door from the inside. These actions could have been done innocently in the first minutes of the search for Madeleine but equally could be seen as deliberate actions to pervert the course of justice. In my book *Vanished – the Truth About the Disappearance of Madeleine McCann* (John Blake Publishing, 2008), I point out that the chief inspector was not made aware at the time of her reported disappearance that the McCanns and some of their friends had deliberately left the rear patio doors of their apartments – approached by a flight of steps from the individual gardens – ajar to allow themselves and other members of the party to take it in turns to check on the children at half-hourly intervals. It was evidently a process that had been tried and tested on a group holiday in Greece the year before.

However, the fact of the open patio door would not be revealed until a week later, the delay in passing on the information caused no doubt by an oversight. That excuse was discarded by Amaral and the eventual disclosure was assumed to be a weak alibi put up after it had been proved evident that the shutters could not be forced open by an intruder from the outside. The innocent McCanns became the prime suspects in a murder that never took place and were eventually declared official suspects in the investigation, a status often conferred under Portuguese law.

The patio door was certainly open when the police arrived. The first officers of the Guarda Nacional Republicana on the scene may have assumed that the simple up-down interior lock on the patio doors would present no insurmountable difficulty to an intelligent and determined three-year-old and that the little girl had wandered out of the apartment in search of her parents. If that were the case, it was likely that she had been picked up by someone in the area and carried away for reasons on which one can only speculate. Much has been made of a paedophile plot hatched to kidnap the personable and attractive young child who had been stalked by the kidnappers for a week before the opportunity arose.

Another theory centred around a local resident, Robert Murat, who was unfortunate to attract the attention of international media on the scene by his constant presence in the area of Waterside Gardens and his apparent willingness to engage investigators in conversation. Murat may have fallen foul of the reports that, ever wise after the event, the UK press had used to point the finger at Soham murderer Ian Huntley, who was also often seen talking to investigators. Mr Murat was an interpreter who often worked with Portimão police and had a more valid reason to be on the scene than the press, but the fact was never allowed to spoil a good story. He was also declared an official suspect, much to the delight of the media circus, although was later cleared of any involvement whatsoever.

Subsequently the police investigation focused on the behaviour of the McCanns and the members of their party during the evening of the child's disappearance. Gerry and Kate McCann had appeared at the poolside restaurant of the Ocean Club at 8.30 pm. Gerry would return to check on his children and those of his friends at 9.00 pm and another of the party would take up the task around 9.30 pm. It would later be suggested by Gerry's recollection of the scene in the apartment that an intruder could have already entered the apartment and was hidden in Madeleine's and the twins' bedroom when Mr McCann stood at the door to check the room. However, he reported feeling no draught, which would have suggested that the window shutter was up and the windows open, and investigators knew that if they were to believe that Madeleine was abducted by an intruder who had entered the apartment, they must also assume that the intruder would follow the criminal pattern and prepare an alternate escape route from the bedroom.

It appeared that DCI Amaral now suspected that the McCanns might have accidentally killed Madeleine, perhaps by an overdose of a tranquilliser, and had hidden her body before raising the alarm. This fanciful theory called for a lengthy stretch of the imagination considering that police dogs were used on the night of the search and one had actually tracked Madeleine up to 400 metres away from the apartment – which suggests that the child had left the apartment of her own volition and wandered in search of her parents. Police accusations against the McCanns became even more preposterous when imported

British police 'cadaver dogs' found evidence of the transportation of Madeleine's 'corpse' in the McCann's hire car, which the McCanns had hired 25 days *after* Madeleine had gone missing. Despite the absurdity of the situation, Portuguese investigators regarded the 'find' as more evidence racked up against the unfortunate parents.

Nonetheless, putting aside the suspicions of Inspector Amaral and his investigating team, it still remained clear that a crime had been committed. The child had not been found and the assumption was that she had been abducted, either from her bedroom – although there was no forensic proof of an intruder's presence – or, more reasonably, off the street. Rumours, aided by the fertile and feverish imaginations of the world's press, abounded: Madeleine had been kidnapped by a Belgian paedophile ring, she was the prisoner of a powerful sheik who kept her as a playmate for his lonely young daughter, or she had been killed by a paedophile who happened to chance upon her as she wandered the street.

The first thought for many was that little Madeleine must have woken up and gone out into the night looking for her parents. The streets were dimly muted in the soft amber streetlights and the beach reflected only the light of the moon and the murmuring of the Atlantic surf. Madeleine McCann was gone.

The rear of apartment blocks 4 and 5 of the Ocean Club's Waterside Garden were outside the complex proper on the other side of the perimeter wall of the pool and restaurant area. To reach them there were two alternate routes. The first was across a grassy area surrounding a small water feature to the left of the large kidney-shaped pool. This led through a large metal gate that gave access to a narrow cobbled walkway that passed along the rear of the apartments. The second, more direct, route passed to the right of the pool through the Ocean Club security gate at the side of the reception building. The walker could then turn left up the hill of Dr Francisco Gentil Martins, following the perimeter wall until it turned sharply to the left at a right angle to form the northern wall of the perimeter, bordering the walkway that ran west to east at the rear of the apartments. Apartment 5A, the McCann's rented apartment where Madeleine, Sean, and Amelie slept, stood on the corner of Block 5 where the walkway abutted the street.

The next door apartment, 5B, was occupied by Russell O'Brien, a member of the McCann party who worked as a consultant in acute medicine at the Royal Devon and Exeter Hospital, and his partner Jane Tanner and their two children. Further down the walkway were the apartments of two more friends of the McCanns, Doctors David and Fiona Payne, where their own offspring slept.

Much debate and criticism has surrounded the distance that the tapas bar, where the parents were dining, lay from the McCanns' corner apartment, and the parents were vilified publicly for leaving the children alone. The circuitous route to the left of the pool was longer at 180 metres but more convenient to check the rear of the apartments where the children of both families slept, a distance to be later ignored by journalists who guesstimated the direct line-of-sight route across the pool from the tapas bar at anything between 40 and 80 metres, not taking into account that anyone pursuing that route would eventually be faced with a climb over a 1.40

metre-high wall as well as a swim across the pool at the start of their journey.

The shorter route through the reception security gate and up the hill was the one sensibly favoured by the McCann party. These areas and the walkway access to the private pool complex were regularly patrolled by Ocean Club security guards.

Dr Matthew Oldfield, who worked at Kingston Hospital in that part of Surrey now swallowed up into South-West London, holidaying with his wife, City headhunter and former lawyer Rachel Oldfield, and their children, checked on all the youngsters at 9.45 pm. He approached the rear-facing apartments that were shrouded from the view of the poolside revellers by a thick hedge of exotic pink-and-white oleander blossoms backed by low bushes and trees that ran along the pool's northern perimeter, effectively cutting off the sight of anyone entering or leaving the apartments by the elevated rear patios.

Amid all the confusion that would later surround the distance from the rear of apartment 5A from the tapas bar, the Ocean Club plan of the Waterside garden complex shows it to be approximately 120 metres. An employee of the Club in Praia da Luz was later asked by reporters if she would be so kind as to check out the security gate approach by walking the route. She timed the walk at 2 minutes and 30 seconds.

On the night of 3 May, Dr Oldfield entered the gate off the walkway into the small rear garden and followed the steps up to his own patio. He then entered his family holiday apartment where he checked that his children were sleeping soundly. He then returned to the lights of the tapas bar by way of the reception security gate after he checked that the children also slept soundly in the McCanns' apartment.

According to his statement given on 4 May to Portuguese police, Russell Oldfield said he took his turn at checking the children at 9.45 pm. He entered the rear garden of apartment 5A and climbed the steps to the rear patio of the apartment. There, he put his ear to the left-hand sliding glass panel and frame to listen for any sound within the rooms. He heard nothing and assumed the children inside slept on undisturbed. He then walked back to the bar and raised his thumb towards his friends, Gerry and Kate McCann, before reclaiming his place at the table.

At the tapas bar the conversation continued and Kate McCann glanced at her watch, noting the time was after 10.00 pm. Her husband Gerry was in the middle of a story involving an incident at the Glenfield Hospital at Leicester where he was employed as a consultant cardiologist. Not wanting to break into his monologue or disturb the company, Kate rose from the table and made her way around the pool and through the security gate to walk up the hill to the apartments.

On reaching the apartment, mounting the steps and sliding open the unlocked patio door, Kate was struck by a sense of stillness. She made her way across the dining area to the front bedroom on the left where she had settled Madeleine and the twins before leaving with Gerry for the restaurant. Now the twins slept on in their cots but Madeleine's bed was empty.

Kate moved quickly through the rooms of the small apartment calling her daughter's name. The twins stirred and began to whimper. Kate frantically checked the bathroom and her own and Gerry's bedroom, pulling up the bedclothes and looking under the bed frame before rooting through wardrobes. Panic overtook her. Her hysterical shouts that someone – 'they' was the word that Charlotte Pennington would recall – had taken her daughter and her repeated cries of Madeleine's name now rising to hysteria brought Charlotte Pennington, a childminder on duty watch in a nearby apartment, to the scene.

Confusion continued to reign as the alerted diners sobered rapidly and found themselves along with staff and residents wandering the nearby streets of the resort calling out the lost child's name. The first thought for many, despite Kate McCann's alleged dramatic outburst to the childminder, was that little Madeleine must have woken up and gone out into the night looking for her parents.

The outcome of this tragic story, a crime with no description and no identified perpetrator, is that there isn't one. According to a multitude of reports, Madeleine McCann had been seen all over the world: in Argentina, Paraguay, the United States, Australia, Morocco, and Holland. There are traces of her everywhere and nowhere. It is a crime that shocked the world because Madeleine disappeared from where all children are deemed to be safe, from her bed at night. Her parents, who have travelled the world to keep alive the search for their daughter, were dining at a restaurant barely two-and-a-half minutes walk from where their children slept. The Portuguese authorities have made it absolutely clear that the couple are no longer regarded as suspects in their daughter's disappearance. One day perhaps the secret of

Madeleine McCann's disappearance will be known. Is her tiny ravaged corpse buried on some barren Portuguese hillside or does she sit in laughing attendance on the beautiful young daughter of a foreign sheik? The world and the McCanns wait.

CHAPTER 9

THE YOUNG HEIRESS

Shropshire, England, 14 January 1975

*'I never killed her; she must have fallen off the shelf
and hung herself'*

– Donald Neilson, speaking to police
after his arrest.

Newspaper reports of crimes can often themselves form the inspiration from which crimes are evolved. So it was in December of 1974 when a man known to the police as 'The Black Panther' read a report in the *Shropshire Star* of the death of George Whittle, a local entrepreneur who had built up a successful coach company operating from Highley, the Whittles' home town, and another in Kidderminster. Whittle had left his 17-year-old daughter Leslie a fortune which the young heiress would receive on reaching 21: the sum of £82,000 – roughly £500,000 by 2009 values. But Leslie was never to celebrate her 21st birthday because the man reading the newspaper was serial-killer Donald Neilson.

Neilson was 39 years old, a self-employed builder from Bradford, West Yorkshire, who had turned to crime when his business failed. He had married in 1955 at the age of 18 and had a daughter Kathryn, but despite those blessings life had not been kind to the future killer, nor was Neilson his birth surname. He had been born Donald Nappey and the name had made him a butt of jokes at school and during National Service in the army. He changed his surname by deed poll when Kathryn started school in 1960, to 'avoid for her the humiliation' he himself had suffered as a child. Those who knew Neilson in those days describe him as a loner, obsessed with army life to the extent that he took his wife and young daughter on self-planned military-type manoeuvres and Spartan-style camping trips. He also had an unhealthy obsession with firearms, of which he had a large collection.

Despite the affectionate feelings he extended towards his daughter, Neilson had no qualms about turning to a life of crime, and investigators into his early career as a petty burglar attributed him with more than 400 house robberies. Takings were low, however, so Neilson acquired a balaclava and a handgun and took to robbing post offices in small towns. By the time he read of Leslie Whittle's inheritance, Neilson had escalated his criminal career to the fatal shootings of three sub-postmasters. His habit of wearing a balaclava to hide his face during the robberies had also earned him the nickname the Black Panther.

After reading of the Whittle inheritance, Neilson, now a wanted man across Britain, began to put together a plan to kidnap the young heiress. Leslie lived at home with her elderly mother and the resistance expected from a 17-year-old girl would be minimal. His housebreaking skills would allow him to enter the unguarded property with ease and should opposition occur from the unexpected presence of Leslie's married brother, 31-year-old Robert, Neilson wouldn't hesitate to shoot to kill. The ransom demanded would be £50,000 with possibly more to come later, but first there was the matter of where the victim would be hidden.

For this, Neilson chose a location that would add to the horror of the crime and shock the public when it was revealed, together with its horrific content. Leslie Whittle would be tethered by a wire around her neck on a ledge in a vertical storm drain in Bathpool Park at Kidsgrove in Staffordshire. Wet, cold, and hungry, and at the mercy of the elements, the young girl would remain captive until her family paid the ransom – or until Neilson felt her captivity no longer served his criminal purpose.

The disappearance of the teenager as her mother slept in a nearby room startled the nation. Mrs Whittle's statement to police recalled that she arrived home at 12.45 am and found her daughter Leslie asleep in bed. Mrs Whittle then took her usual sleeping tablet and slept heavily, awakening at 7.00 am when she bathed and went down to the kitchen to prepare Leslie's breakfast. When her daughter hadn't come down for breakfast – it was a Tuesday and Leslie was due to attend Wulfrun Campus, Wolverhampton College, where she was enrolled as a student – Mrs Whittle went to her room and was surprised to find that her daughter was not in bed. Her clothes for that day were neatly stacked on a chair. In a panic, Leslie's mother picked up the telephone to call her son Ronald but found the phone was dead. Still wearing her dressing gown, the distraught woman ran to the door in the lounge that connected with the adjoining garage and found it open, although it was always kept locked, she insisted to police.

After driving frantically to alert her son and his wife, she returned with the couple and together they searched the house. In the lounge, placed on the carpet in front of the fireplace, they found a box of Turkish delight. Inside the box was a ransom demand for £50,000 along with instructions for a family member to be at a certain telephone box at a certain time to receive instructions on how the ransom was to be paid.

A check of Leslie's wardrobe revealed that only her dressing gown and her bedroom slippers were missing. Despite a warning contained in the note, Ronald Whittle telephoned the police. A press blackout descended on the investigation while the police waited for word from the kidnapper. Huge reinforcements of police were drafted into the area of the search, which extended across three counties. Roadblocks were set up on all major roads and members of the public were questioned as police made door-to-door enquiries. Detectives were hampered by having no timeline of the kidnapping.

Leslie Whittle had disappeared from her bed sometime between 12.45 am and 7.00 am during the night of 14 January, and there were no eyewitnesses to her departure. Various scenarios were considered including the possibility that she had simply run away from home. And as is usual in such cases, her boyfriend was viewed as a possible suspect, perhaps in a ruse to prematurely obtain money from Leslie's trust fund. But police enquiries took on another focus when her brother Ronald's trips to the telephone box were rewarded on 16 January at 11.30 pm when a recorded voice tape from Leslie assured her family that she was in good health and that a member of her family should go to a telephone box in Kidsgrove where further instructions would be found hidden behind the backboard of the kiosk.

From thereon the tragic circumstances of the case developed into a black comedy as police took two hours to arrange a plan to track the kidnapper. On his way to Kidsgrove, Ronald Whittle took a wrong turning in the dark and arrived late at the telephone box outside Kidsgrove post office. After a fumbling 30 minute search of the backboard he located a message that told him to drive to Bathpool Park, one-and-a-half miles away. There he again became lost and failed to give a pre-arranged signal by flashing his light at a designated point in the park. The dejected brother met up with police, who later searched the park with no success.

The news blackout on the Whittle kidnapping was lifted on 10 February and an interview on television between Ron Whittle and the police led to a mention of Bathpool Park, which immediately brought a response from the public. A local schoolteacher contacted police to tell of two discoveries by his pupils. The first was of Dymo labels (a type of hand impression tape printer popular in the Seventies), which read 'Drop suitcase into hole'. Their second discovery was of a torch wedged into the grille of a capped ventilation shaft. The shaft was one of three, of which the largest had originally ventilated the now defunct Nelson Coal Mine.

The first two shafts were uncapped and a search of the

first revealed only a Dymo impressing machine and a roll of the distinctive metal tape. The second shaft was empty. The third shaft, uncapped on 7 March, was left for 24 hours because of a possible gas hazard and searched the next day. The Nelson ventilation shaft extended 61 feet down to link with the coalmine's ventilation system. A first inspection revealed a ladder leading down to a ledge 22 feet below the surface. The ledge was empty but 23 feet below was another landing where police found a tape recorder. On a third lower ledge, this at 54 feet below ground, the searchers' torches illuminated a sleeping bag, a yellow foam mattress, and a survival blanket. A grim discovery awaited them. Hanging suspended from the ledge by a steel wire around her neck was the body of 17-year-old Leslie Whittle, clad still in her dirty bathrobe. Her slippers were lying amid detritus on the floor just seven inches below her outstretched feet. From the ledge to the floor measured just seven feet. Leslie Whittle had slowly strangled to death, presumably pushed from the ledge by Neilson after the first bungled ransom attempt. Also amid the rubbish on the floor were strips of three-inch-wide Elastoplast that had been used as a blindfold and gag, a pair of men's size 7 brown trainers, more Dymotape, a thermos flask, a cassette tape, microphone and leads as well as a pair of men's blue cord trousers and a notepad – blank but containing a partial fingerprint. However, the fingerprint yielded no match on the national police database and the search for Leslie Whittle's kidnapper and murderer lost momentum.

The eventual breakthrough wouldn't come for another nine months, when two alert police constables on patrol in their car in Mansfield on 11 December noticed a man acting suspiciously near a post office. As the police car approached, the man ducked his head in an effort to hide his face and walked away at speed. When stopped and questioned he gave his name as 'John Moxon' before pulling a sawn-off shotgun from under his coat and ordering the two surprised policemen into his car where he told them to drive him to the nearby village of Blidworth.

During the tense drive, during which the gunman sat behind the driver and kept the muzzle of the shotgun pressed against the officer's back, it became apparent to both policemen that they were going to be killed as soon as they reached their destination. No desperate gunman with obvious 'form' would allow them to live after having seen his face. 'John Moxon' was planning their death.

In the front passenger seat the second officer kept a 180-degree watch on the shotgun muzzle, waiting for it to waver, and as the car was forced to brake suddenly at a road junction into the village he saw the shotgun swing off aim. With a shout to his partner to beware, he threw himself across the back seat and tackled the gunman as the car slewed into the narrow village High Street and stopped before a fish shop. Becoming aware of the death struggle before them, several brawny miners outside the shop rushed to the officers' assistance and eventually the officers found themselves protecting the battered gunman from the fury of the mob.

At the police station in Mansfield, the duty sergeant who searched Moxon was surprised to find the man carried a duplicate of everything, right down to two perfectly synchronised watches, two torches, two batteries, and two knives. They also found two balaclavas and began to suspect that they had caught the elusive Black Panther. The prisoner, however, refused to answer questions on the pretext of protecting his wife and daughter. Not until he was told that his photograph would be circulated to the press to aid identification did he identify himself as 'Donald Neilson of Grangefield Avenue, Leeds'. The thunderbolt was yet to fall. Fingerprints sent for identification matched Neilson to the partial print found on the reporter's notebook at the Leslie Whittle crime scene. After nine months of fruitless searching, the police had got their man.

Donald Neilson went on trial at Oxford Crown Court on 14 June 1976, charged with the murders of three sub-postmasters and the kidnap and murder of Leslie Whittle. Other charges included grievous bodily harm to the wife of one of the murdered men, burglary, and firearm charges. He was found guilty by a unanimous jury and condemned to four sentences of life imprisonment. Originally sentenced to a minimum of 30 years, which saw him liable for parole in 2006 when he was 70, Neilson's application has been turned down at various times since, and he has been told that the severity of his crimes warrants imprisonment until death. He is imprisoned at HMP Norwich and is reported to be suffering from progressive and fatal motor neurone disease. Neilson appealed his convictions for the murders of Leslie Wittle and the sub-postmasters in 2007 when he claimed that Leslie Whittle slipped from the ledge and that the post-office killings were all accidents. His appeal was refused.

CHAPTER 10

THE VIRGINIA
TECH MASSACRE

Blacksburg, Virginia, USA, 16 April 2007

'I didn't have to do this; I could have left'
— Seung-Hui Cho, in a note left for police.

Seung-Hui Cho, who preferred the Western order of the surname placed after the Christian name, was a senior undergraduate student at Virginia Tech in Blacksburg, Virginia, when the massacre occurred. Cho was born in Seoul, South Korea, and arrived in the United States when his family emigrated to Detroit in 1992 before joining the large ethnic Korean community that had settled in North Virginia over the years. He eventually became a US permanent resident while retaining his South Korean citizenship. Such a status does not particularly indicate the nationalistic leanings of the subject but is rather a requirement under South Korean law, which does not permit dual nationality for its citizens living or working abroad.

While still at school he began to demonstrate occasional

bouts of depressive behaviour and was eventually diagnosed with a severe anxiety disorder, identified as selective mutism. The condition is rooted in childhood trauma and is apparent when a person who is normally capable of speech is unable to speak in given situations or to specific people. Selective mutism is a recently recognised condition that was once – and probably still is in certain areas of society such as schools and the armed services – looked on with derision as the subject becomes more and more tongue-tied.

Following the diagnosis, Cho began to receive treatment and therapy together with special education support until his junior year of high school. However, during what would become his last two years at Virginia Tech, his behaviour was becoming increasingly aberrant and plays and essays he submitted to his teachers showed marked referrals to violent behaviour, causing concern among the academic staff and classmates. Following the events of 16 April, 2007, strong criticism would emerge from a panel set up by Virginia Governor Tim Kaine to investigate the massacre. Educators and mental health staff professionals who had come into contact with Cho during his college years were especially seen at fault in their failure to recognise his deteriorating condition. Glaring flaws in the state's mental health system and gun laws were also highlighted. In particular, the media would seize on failings of college officials and security to take immediate action to warn students after the first bout of shootings.

Certainly, concerns about Seung-Hui Cho's behaviour were common during his early childhood in South Korea, where relatives had formed the opinion that the morose child was either a mute or mentally ill. Cho seldom spoke and refused to play with other children, preferring to sit alone in a corner and avoid all human contact. When called upon by his parents, however, the child would readily obey verbal commands and showed respect towards his elders. A worrying factor was the boy's hatred of school, often returning home to the basement apartment that was the family home in Seoul where he would hurl his books to the floor and go into a tantrum. 'Cho hated school,' his grandfather told reporters when interviewed after the massacre.

In the United States, Cho studied at the Poplar Tree Elementary School in Chantilly and completed the school's three-year program in just 18 months, proving himself to be a highly proficient student. According to classmates and staff he was 'highly intelligent, a good dresser, and popular with the girls'. However, the deterioration in his mental condition would be noted as he moved through Ormond Stone Middle School in Centreville and Westfield High School in Chantilly. By the eighth grade he was again violently expressing his hatred of school and suffering from bouts of selective mutism, leading to teasing by his classmates that would fuel the fire of the slayings at Virginia Tech. Jokes would also be made at his expense because of his poor and accented English stemming from a home atmosphere in which all family members spoke their native Korean. 'He was often told to go back to China,' said one student. 'Nobody liked him because he was weird and always wanted to be alone. If someone tried to speak to him he'd either clam up or answer in a strange, deep voice that sounded like he was underwater...'

Cho graduated from Westfield High School in 2003. A clear warning of what was to come went unnoticed in 1999, the year of the Columbine High School massacre in Colorado when students Eric Harris and Dylan Klebold shot and killed 12 students and a teacher, injuring 24 others before committing suicide. A fellow student of the then 15-year-old Cho recalled the Korean youth becoming 'transfixed' at the news. 'I remember sitting next to him in Spanish class and there was something written on his folder to the effect of "Fuck you all, I hope you all burn in hell".' Cho also wrote in a school essay of his desire to 'repeat Columbine'. The school contacted Cho's sister who reported the incident to her parents. Cho was sent to a psychiatrist.

What seems strange in the various diagnoses put forward by the mental health professionals with access to the troubled student is that nowhere is there a mention of autism. Such speculation would arise only after the event and the outpouring of grief that would shake America and the world. Although autistic children and adults are not generally given to violence, limited data suggests that in certain conditions, particular forms of autism can lead to acts of violence and aggression in which the affected individual demonstrates psychotic behaviour with no consideration for the victim. Any such information concerning Seung-Hui Cho's mental condition passed on to Virginia Tech may have served as an alert to the possible future behaviour of the troubled student and led to a more vigorous action by college security staff in the early hours of Cho's killing spree. But federal law forbids the disclosure of any record of disability or treatment of an individual without the subject's express permission.

Westfield officials, therefore, disclosed none of Cho's anxiety-related problems or deep-rooted aggression to Virginia Tech.

In his freshman year Cho originally enrolled at Virginia Tech – officially Virginia Polytechnic Institute and State University – as an undergraduate major in business information technology, involving computer science and management coursework, but by his senior year he had changed his coursework to English major. 'Major' indicates the main course chosen by the undergraduate in which he hopes to receive the equivalent of a British degree or pass.

By his senior year Cho's behaviour was becoming more and more unusual. Poet and academic Nikki Giovanni, who taught poetry at Virginia High, recollects that she had Cho removed from her class because she found his behaviour 'menacing'. His writing, recalls Giovanni, was 'intimidating' as was his recently formed habit of photographing female students' legs under their desks and distributing obscene and violent poetry. Alarmed at the Korean student's behaviour, department head Lucinda Roy alerted the students' affairs office, the dean's office, and the campus police, but each responded that they could do nothing unless Cho made overt threats against himself or others.

However, the campus police were required to act in 2005 when they had cause to issue Cho with two verbal warnings regarding stalking incidents on campus. A female student reported that Cho had visited her room uninvited, wearing sunglasses and behaving in an arrogant and obnoxious manner. His behaviour was threatening enough for the girl to call campus police who later visited Cho in his dormitory and warned him not to bother the girl again.

Cho complied but below the surface his anger at the rejection was seething. Soon after, he switched his attention to another female student who contacted campus police after a colleague warned her that Cho was 'schizophrenic'. Again Cho complied with a warning from the campus police and later e-mailed a classmate that he was considering suicide. Campus authorities were notified and Cho was escorted to the New River Valley Community Services Board, the Virginia state mental health facility serving the area of Blacksburg. On 13 December 2005 Cho was found to be mentally ill and in need of hospitalisation. He was detained temporarily at Carillon St Albans Behavioural Health Centre in Radford, Virginia, pending a committal hearing.

At the hearing, Special Justice Paul Barnett certified that Seung-Hui Cho 'presented an imminent danger to himself as a result of mental illness' but instead of committing Cho, Justice Barnett recommended treatment as an outpatient. Although the recommendation carried a rider that Cho was to follow all recommended treatments, the result was that Seung-Hui Cho was not committed, which meant that, under Virginia state law, the mentally ill young man was eligible to buy firearms.

Some law experts would later argue that the blame for allowing Cho to arm himself rested with the state police, who had the responsibility of checking all applications to buy arms against their list of prohibited persons on which Cho should have figured, having been judged as a mental defective. The decision not to commit the mentally unstable student meant that his name was not registered with the authorities. The omission was to cost the lives of 32 people.

Early in 2007, as Cho's delusionary behaviour grew worse and he began to feel threatened and insecure on the campus, he began to build up an arsenal of weapons. In February he bought a .22 Walther P22 semi-automatic pistol through the Internet. The gun was shipped to a gun dealer where Cho had completed the necessary forms for purchase and there he took possession of the weapon. This was followed by the purchase of a 9 mm Glock 19 pistol, magazines for both pistols, and hollow-point ammunition. He practised with both handguns at a shooting range 40 miles from campus and staff there would later recall the dour-faced Oriental 'youth' – Cho was 23 – who spoke to no one before entering the booth, where he fired hails of bullets and expended massive amounts of rounds in an orgy of shooting at the tattered targets.

At approximately 7.15 am on the morning of 16 April 2007, the fourth floor of the West Ambler Johnston Hall dormitory block echoed to the sound of gunfire. Ryan Clark, a male resident assistant working in the co-educational wing, followed the sound of shots to the room occupied by Emily Hilscher, a 19-year-old freshman, and found the girl slumped on the bed, bleeding from wounds to the chest and head. Seung-Hui Cho, wearing dark trousers and a black windbreaker and hung with two crossed shoulder holsters, stood over the dying girl, brandishing two handguns. As Clark went to the girl's assistance, Cho shot him dead. Speculation would later arise that Cho was obsessed with his first victim and had become enraged when she rejected his advances, although this has never been confirmed.

Cho then calmly strolled past horrified onlookers and returned to his own dormitory in nearby Harper Hall that he shared with four other senior undergraduates. There he changed out of his blood-spattered clothing, reloaded the pistols, and deleted his e-mails from his personal computer before removing the hard drive. All this occurred while police and medical staff responded to the scene of the shooting close by and pandemonium raged in the building.

Two hours later, still unchallenged as police scoured the university grounds, Cho emerged from the building and went to a local post office where he mailed a package to NBC News. The package contained some photographs, written documents and a video of Cho posing with his firearms. A photograph of a soft-nosed bullet carried the caption: 'All the shit you've given me, right back at you with hollow points.' Two and a half hours after the first shootings, Cho was seen crossing the campus to the classrooms at Norris Hall wearing a backpack, later found to contain chains, locks, a hammer, a knife, the two pistols, 19 loaded magazines and 400 rounds of ammunition. Students attending classes in Norris Hall were unaware of the spectre stalking them, since no alert had been issued following the West Ambler Johnston dormitory slayings.

Once inside the building Cho used the locks and chains to secure the three main entrance doors. Methodically, the young killer took the stairway to the second floor and began to search classrooms for particular victims, appearing at doorways and peering into individual classrooms. Eventually he entered an advanced hydrology engineering class and shot dead the startled professor, G V Loganathan. He then turned both guns on the class of 13 and killed nine, leaving two injured and two unscathed. In an adjoining classroom, lecturer Chris Bishop was taking a class in German. He and six of his students died in a hail of bullets which also left six wounded.

The sounds of gunshots and the screams of the wounded prompted students in other classrooms into action and they began to barricade doors. A hero of the massacre appeared in the form of Professor Liviu Librescu, a 76-year-old Romanian Jew who had survived the Holocaust in Eastern Europe. The frail academic threw himself against the barricaded door and used his body to prevent Cho entering as his students escaped by jumping from the windows. All but one had made their escape by the time the professor succumbed to the many gunshot wounds he had sustained as the enraged Cho fired shot after shot through the door. Both the remaining student and Professor Librescu died. In room 211, teacher Jocelyne Couture-Nowak and a student, Henry Lee, also died heroes' deaths as they fought to keep Cho from entering the classroom.

Standing in the corridor amid the blood and carnage Cho reloaded and began another prowl through the classrooms littered with the dead and the dying. At room 206 Cho fired through the door and wounded students Katelyn Carney and Derek O'Dell as they manned a hastily erected barricade. Other students died in individual acts of heroism as they protected their wounded colleagues from the blood-crazed killer. Student Zach Petkewicz saved his classmates by barricading the door with a large oak table and holding it wedged in position despite the shots that the foiled gunman fired through the door. Professor Kevin Granata, teaching on the floor above, locked his class of 20 students into an office before going downstairs to investigate the shootings. He was fatally shot down by Cho. None of his students were injured.

The blood bath lasted for 12 minutes before Seung-Hui Cho ended the slaughter by shooting himself in the head with the 9 mm Glock 19, the hollow-point soft-nosed bullet destroying his face and causing investigators to resort to fingerprinting for identification. In those 12 minutes, Cho had murdered 30 people and wounded 17. He had fired his pistols at least 174 times, an estimate based on the number of unused live rounds found in his backpack. Six students suffered injuries when they jumped from the second-storey windows as the heroic Professor Librescu held the attacker at bay.

Confusion was rife on the campus as local and state police directed medical teams into the building after breaking through the chained and locked doors and confirming that the gunman had worked alone. They were appalled at what they found; the lifeblood of fatally wounded victims literally swamped the floor and barricaded doors made access difficult on the second floor. Once the identity of the dead gunman had been confirmed – some students had recognised the Korean when he burst into their classroom – a search of his dormitory found a note written by Cho in which he criticised 'rich kids' as 'deceitful and debauched charlatans'. He also laid the blame for his actions on his victims, adding in a postscript: 'You made me do this'.

A criminal investigation later confirmed that Cho had used the heavier 9 mm Glock 19 in most of the killings in the Norris Hall classrooms, although some victims bore superficial wounds from the Walther .22. Emily Hilscher and Ryan Clark had also been killed with the Glock 19. Scene-of-Crime officers recovered at least 17, 10 and 15 capacity empty magazines scattered around the bloodied classrooms. As the investigation proceeded detectives became more and more convinced that Cho had been selecting his victims and planning the shootings for several months. Belatedly, detectives also discovered that the killer had never complied with Justice Paul Barnett's order to undergo outpatient mental treatment. Accusations flew back and forth as various departments involved in Cho's original assessment denied responsibility for his supervision and passed the buck between them.

Christopher Flynn, chief student counsellor at Virginia High, summed up the flaws in the bureaucracy involved when he told the court of inquiry: 'When a court gives a mandatory order that someone is to get outpatient treatment, that order is to the individual, not an agency such as the college counselling centre. The ones responsible for ensuring that the mentally ill person receives help in these sorts of cases are the mentally ill persons themselves.'

Virginia law does stipulate that if a person fails to comply with a court order to seek mental health treatment as an outpatient, they can be brought back to the court for assessment and committed to an institution for mandatory treatment for up to six months, but Cho's case had obviously been overlooked, with tragic consequences.

Two days after the shootings the package mailed by Cho arrived at the offices of NBC News in New York. Inside, the killer had placed video clips, photographs and a document explaining the reasons for his actions. A controversial decision was made to release excerpts from the tapes, and concern was expressed by families of the victims that allowing Cho to speak of his venom through the media could lead to copycat killings. There have been 16 school shootings recorded in the USA since Virginia High, which have claimed a total of 21 victims, but none with the severity of the Virginia High Massacre.

There is no doubt however, that Cho was himself influenced by the Columbine School killers Eric Harris and Dylan Klebold, whose names were contained in documents sent to NBC News. In another, Cho appeared to blame his victims for the pain inflicted by suppressive regimes like that of Pol Pot in Cambodia. The document read: '*Do you know what it feels to be spit on your face and to have trash shoved down your throat? Do you know what it feels like to dig your own grave? Do you know what it feels like to have your throat slashed from ear to ear? Do you know what it feels like to be torched alive? Do you know what it feels like to be humiliated and be impaled (on) upon a cross? And left to bleed to death for your amusement? You have never felt a single ounce of pain your whole life. Did you want to inject as much misery in our lives as you can just because you can? I didn't have to do this. I could have left. I could have fled. But no, I will no longer run. It's not for me. For my children, for my brothers and sisters that you fucked, I did it for them. When the time came, I did it. I had to. You had a hundred billion chances and ways to have avoided today, but you decided to spill my blood. You forced me into a corner and gave me only one option. The decision was yours. Now you have blood on your hands that will never wash off.'*

CHAPTER 11

THE COLUMBINE HIGH
SCHOOL MASSACRE

Colorado, USA, 20 April 1999

'Peek-a- boo!'
— Shooter Dylan Klebold, to students attempting
to hide under a table.

Eight years before the mentally ill Korean undergraduate Seung-Hui Cho went on his rampage at
Virginia High, the massacre that may have ignited Cho's
feverish mind to murder occurred further south, in the
state of Colorado. There, in a corner where Jefferson
County meets its border with Arapahoe County, two
teenage students of the Columbine High School went on a
rampage of death and destruction armed with handguns,
rifle, shotguns, and home-made bombs.

Eric David Harris, who had just turned 18, and Dylan
Bennet Klebold (17) usually spent their evenings working
at the town's Blackjack Pizzas, where they heated up
orders for takeaway and inside eating, but on 19 April the
teenagers had other things on their minds. Harris was the

shorter of the two, a clean-cut teenager with a buzz-top haircut and a ready smile who attracted the duller Klebold to his company. Klebold was a gangling youth with a large nose and mouse-coloured hair, parted in the middle, that constantly flopped across his forehead. Both were angry at their high school classmates and Klebold especially suffered from a deep manic depression that cast an unwelcome influence on the already unstable Harris, who was himself on medication for depression and feelings of uncontrollable anger.

Both felt that the world had let them down and had often contemplated a joint suicide but of late the thought had expanded into taking as many of their hated schoolmates and teachers with them as possible. They had both scoured the Internet for bomb-making procedures and had built up an arsenal of primed butane canisters, pipe bombs, and small hand-thrown devices. In the months prior to the attack both boys had acquired a collection of unlicensed firearms bought from older acquaintances.

Their arsenal of weapons included two 9 mm semi-automatic pistols, two 12-gauge shotguns, and a 9 mm carbine. The butts and barrels of the shotguns had been sawn off to make it easier to conceal them under the long, black trench coats that the boys habitually wore, earning them the title among schoolmates as The Trench Coat Mafia. The day chosen for their revenge on society was the next day, 20 April, coincidentally or possibly by design, the 110th anniversary of the birth of Adolf Hitler.

At 11.10 am on the day of the massacre Harris and Klebold arrived in separate cars, Harris turning left into the Junior Student parking area and Klebold turning right into the Senior Students' lot. Although both teenagers were senior students neither parked in the space allotted to them, their plan being to flank the school before making their entry. Earlier they had driven to a playing field half a mile away where they set up two butane canister bombs wired to detonate at 11.19 am, two minutes after two similar bombs that they planned to plant in the school canteen. The plan was to take up positions near their flanking automobiles and shoot any survivors of the explosion as they fled the building. The teenagers had recently confirmed that from 11.15 am, the time of the mid-morning break, the canteen would be at its fullest, almost 500 students and staff relaxing over their coffee and biscuits. The detonation of the canisters planted in the field was intended to divert emergency services responding to the school bombing.

Their plans were temporarily foiled when both canteen bombs failed to detonate at the allotted time. It was later assessed by bomb disposal experts that each canister contained enough home-made explosive to bring down the entire canteen and the library above, killing everyone within the blast area. Following their temporary confusion when the bombs failed to explode, the soon-to-be-killers met at the top of a landscaped staircase near the high school's west entrance and considered their alternatives.

An explosion from the field where they had planted the earlier bombs seemed to galvanise them both into action. With a shout of 'Go! Go!' from Eric Harris, both pulled out their shotguns from under their trench coats and began shooting at students grouped near the entrance. Rachel Scott, a pretty dark-haired 17-year-old, was the first to die, shot in the head, chest, and leg. Richard Castaldo, her companion with whom she had been sharing her mid-morning break, was hit eight times by the 00 gauge buckshot and collapsed to the ground seriously wounded.

The silence that followed the first outburst of shooting was profound as students struggled to understand what was happening. Many remained where they stood, believing they were witnessing a school stunt staged by senior students who would be leaving at the end of the term. Such events were not unusual and a scattered clapping was joined by a few muted cheers before the killers shrugged off their trench coats and drew handguns which they turned on the crowd. Daniel Rohrbough, Sean Graves, and Lance Kirklin were shot as they innocently walked up the steps where the gunmen stood. All fell wounded to the ground but were spared as Harris and Klebold turned and directed their lethal fire towards groups of students sitting on a grassy bank opposite the school entrance.

Pandemonium erupted as blood erupted from the victims and it became apparent that the students were witnessing a bloody slaughter. Sixteen-year-old Mike Johnson was hit but kept running away from the danger, but his companion Mark Taylor was less fortunate as a bullet struck him in the upper thigh, shattering the femur and causing him to collapse, crippled, to the ground. As he heard Harris and Klebold approach and the click of a loading magazine, the wounded boy clenched his eyes shut and played dead. Then remembering that he had read somewhere that people died with their eyes open, he opened his eyes and saw Klebold glance his way as he and Harris walked by, laughing and brandishing their pistols.

Mark Taylor's quick thinking saved his life and he survived until medical help arrived after the killers had re-entered the school building.

Klebold and Harris entered the canteen, coming upon two of their earlier victims who had attempted to seek refuge in the building after being wounded by the duo outside. Daniel Rohrbough was shot in the back by Klebold and fell dead. Lance Kirklin had already collapsed and now was lying helpless next to Rohrbough's body. In passing, Klebold casually pointed his pistol downwards and shot Kirklin in the face. He continued into the canteen, stepping over Sean Graves who lay at the entrance. Harris entered behind Klebold, shooting at several students who sat frozen in fear near the canteen doors.

Eye witnesses among the survivors would afterwards tell of Klebold's peculiar manner of rapping on tables under which students cowered and calling out 'Peek-a-boo!' before firing several times under the table at point-blank range into the terrified groups. They then left the building again, scattering pipe bombs and hand devices as they went, few of which actually detonated.

The first alert to police of the shootings was logged at 11.25 am, after teacher Patti Nielson, hearing the commotion from inside the building, had run towards the interior west entrance doors expecting to disrupt a noisy senior student stunt. She was accompanied by senior student Brian Anderson. As the teacher and student approached the doors, the windows exploded inwards, shot out by Harris and Klebold. Patti Nielson was cut by flying glass and Brian Anderson fell wounded between the interior and exterior doors. The injured teacher, bleeding from cuts, staggered back down the hall to the library, where she alerted students to conceal themselves before dialling 911.

Within five minutes a Jefferson County deputy sheriff was on the scene and engaged the killers with gunfire as they made to enter the building where the injured Brian Anderson was lying. The exposed killers turned and returned fire at the deputy who radioed out a Code 33 'officer in need of emergency assistance' call. After emptying his magazine at the deputy, Harris followed Klebold back into the school. Anderson, meanwhile, had dragged himself to the library where he lay bleeding until found by emergency services hours later.

Once back inside the building, the blood-crazed teenagers made for the school's east entrance, shooting anyone they found in their path, turned back to the west entrance and from there to the Library Hall. Coach Dave Sanders, who had just completed evacuating the canteen by way of a staircase up to the second floor, was just descending, accompanied by a male student, to search for additional victims and to evacuate the library area. The staircase was located in the corridor next to the Library Hall and as coach and student turned a corner they almost collided with Klebold and Harris coming the other way. Both killers opened fire as Coach Sanders and the student fled. Dylan Klebold opened fire with his handgun, hitting Sanders in the back, shoulders, head and neck, four of the heavy 9 mm bullets exiting through his chest. The accompanying student made it unscathed to a classroom where he alerted the teacher.

Sanders, meanwhile, managed to stagger to another classroom where 30 students had been taking an examination. They barricaded the doors and placed a sign in the window that read, 'One bleeding to death'. Meanwhile, male students stripped off their shirts and attempted to stem the flow of blood from the dying man's chest, neck, and head wounds. While emergency medical services gave instructions via a telephone link, the coach's condition failed to improve. Students were finally evacuated through a classroom window but Coach Sanders's condition was judged too delicate to move him. He died of massive blood loss at 3 pm. A later examination of the canteen CCTV showed Coach Sanders leaping to his feet and making for the stairs to upper floors to warn students as Harris and Klebold entered, firing their weapons. Dave Sanders was the only member of staff to die in the massacre.

But Klebold and Harris were not yet finished. Entering the Library Hall, Harris shot out a display case and yelled for all of 52 students and their two accompanying teachers lying under tables to 'Get up!' Harris had a particular hatred of school athletes, referred to as 'jocks' in American schools and colleges. In popular fiction these are the muscular, handsome guys who always get the girl – perhaps Harris believed that too.

'All jocks stand up! We'll get the guys in white hats!' Harris shouted loudly, referring to the Columbine tradition of sports team members wearing distinctive white baseball caps. Wisely, no one stood up and Harris was heard to mutter: 'Fine, I'll start anyway.' He and Klebold then moved to the shattered windows and fired out at the police before turning to fire into the room. Kyle Velásquez, a young student hiding under a computer table, was killed by shots to the head and back.

The murderous pair then turned their attention to the windows, from where they noticed police evacuating students from other parts of the building. They exchanged fire with the officers for some minutes before Harris resumed shooting below the tables, imitating Klebold's earlier shouts of 'peek-a-boo!' before firing indiscriminately and discharging his shotgun at the cowering figures hiding beneath. It was here in the Library Hall that the massacre reached its climax as the two killers, by now aware that they would never leave the school alive, began to taunt their intended victims, asking each one individually to plead for his or her life before shooting them down without mercy.

Harris was now bleeding heavily from his nose, which had been broken by the recoil of his shotgun when he had shot under the tables. The pain had put him in an even fouler temper as he joined Klebold in pulling popular school athletes Isaiah Shoels, Matthew Kechter, and Craig Scott out from where they had hidden. Together they spat racial taunts at Shoels before blasting him and Kechter. Craig Scott lay soaking in his friends' blood and pretended to be dead. The killers continued to roam the Library Hall, taunting their victims with words and kicks before shooting them dead.

When they left and paused to reload their weapons, recorded on CCTV as 11.37 am, Klebold called out a student named John Savage, who was an acquaintance. Savage asked what they were doing and Klebold grinned oddly. 'Oh, just killing people,' he replied. He allowed Savage to flee the Library Hall before he and Harris opened fire on the remaining crouching students, at one point shooting up the computer terminal on the bureau directly above where teacher Patti Nielson hid in fear for her life.

The two blood-spattered killers left the Library Hall, laughing, at 11.42 am. Harris's nose was still bleeding and he was heard to remark that he was 'tired of shooting people' to which Klebold replied, 'Perhaps we should knife them – it'd be more fun.' As they left the Hall, 34 uninjured students hurried to get out themselves and to help 10 wounded escape through the north door, which led out onto the paved walk near the west entrance. Patti Nielson emerged and joined Brian Anderson and three library staff in an adjoining break room, where they remained locked in until police entered the building at 3.30 pm.

A CCTV camera recorded the killers back in the canteen at 20 seconds past 11.57 am. Harris is clad in a white T-shirt and dark trousers, holding a 9 mm Hi-Point 995 carbine at his side. He is wearing braces, possibly to support the weight of the ammunition belt and pouches that are shown fastened around his waist. Klebold is caught in motion, walking towards him. He wears grey cargo trousers and a black T-shirt with a black baseball cap worn in reversed fashion on his head. In his left hand he grasps a 9 mm TEC-DC9 pistol with an extended magazine. Klebold wears a black glove on his left hand, Harris wears the other glove of the pair on his right.

Harris is recorded firing a shot from the carbine at one of the unexploded canister bombs in an unsuccessful effort to detonate it. He then takes a sip from a bottle left by a fleeing student as Klebold lights a Molotov cocktail from his backpack and hurls it at the canister. The Molotov cocktail explodes, setting off the water sprinklers, and both killers leave the canteen to head back upstairs. There they appear to wander aimlessly around the corridors, firing desultory shots at the walls and doors. They are aware of students hiding in classrooms behind barricaded doors and look through the window panels to make eye contact but they do not attempt entry. Occasionally they taunt the terrified occupants of locked ' rooms and cubicles, threatening to enter and kill them, but the blood lust seems to have waned.

The duo eventually returned to the Library where two of their earlier victims lay unconscious. Patrick Ireland had been shot twice in the head by Klebold, and Lisa Kreutz, another Klebold victim, had received incapacitating wounds to the body and had not been able to flee the Hall earlier with other students. The bodies of others, shot dead by Klebold and Harris in their last rampage through the Library Hall, were lying scattered nearby.

After firing more rounds at police through the west window, the pair moved to where Isaiah Shoels and Matthew Kechter lay dead and shot themselves without exchanging a word. Eric Harris died by putting his shotgun into his mouth and pulling the trigger, effectively taking off the top of his head. Dylan Klebold shot himself in the head with the 9 mm pistol. Their deaths were recorded by CCTV at 12.08 pm. As the echo of the final shots resounded around the Library Hall, Patrick Ireland temporarily regained consciousness and realised the terror was over before slipping back into darkness. When he recovered consciousness two-and-a-half hours later he managed to crawl to the windows, from which he fell into the arms of a SWAT team member. Lisa Kreutz remained on the library floor until police entered at 3.22 pm, the delay caused by the need for bomb disposal officers to search the building for un-exploded ordnance.

At approximately 1.00 pm, two SWAT teams entered the building, rescuing hidden students and faculty members and taking them to safety. Many of the wounded were taken to nearby hospitals by ambulance and treated for their injuries, while surviving students, teachers, and school assistants were given medical care before being questioned and then bussed to an elementary school at nearby Leawood to be claimed by their families. By 4.30 pm local sheriff John Stone declared the school safe but changed his mind an hour later when explosives were discovered in the car park.

A bomb left in Klebold's car exploded when an officer attempted to defuse the device, leading to the entire school and area being declared a crime scene that night. The building would remain behind police tape until the next morning when a thorough search would be made of the interior. Based on reports by parents who could not find their children among the survivors, Sheriff Stone estimated that 25 students had died in the massacre, a figure that was later amended to 12 students and one teacher, the courageous games coach David Sanders. Twenty-one students were injured by gunfire and three sustained injuries while attempting to escape.

The Columbine High School Massacre is currently rated as the fourth deadliest school massacre in the history of the United States, ranked only below the Bath School Bombing in Michigan in 1927 that killed 45 and injured 58, the Virginia Tech Massacre in 2007, and the University of Texas Massacre of 1966, when crazed sniper Charles Joseph Whitman opened fire from the University tower, killing 14 people and wounding 32 others. The Columbine High School shooting is also regarded as the deadliest attack in an American high school.

CHAPTER 12

DEATH IN HUNGERFORD

Hungerford, Berkshire, England, 19 August 1987

'I wish I'd stayed in bed'
> – Michael Ryan, to a police negotiator.

On 19 August 1987, I stood with my wife and a business partner outside a public house that we had just viewed in the village of Fovant, Wiltshire. It was one of many that we had considered to buy over that month and we were tired of landlords, over-eager to sell and rid themselves of a failing business venture, telling us how successful they'd been and how lucky we were to have such wealth within our grasp.

As I said, we were tired and frankly this one didn't look that bad. The pub was set on the main village street with ample parking and a large barn for functions that already hosted skittles and darts tournaments. We were tempted. Our next appointment to view was a pub in the village of Hungerford, 40 minutes drive away over the county border into West Berkshire. The time was 12.00 pm.

Thirty miles away in the Savernake Forest in Wiltshire, an angry young man named Michael Robert Ryan was wandering through the trees and undergrowth playing his favourite fantasy game in which, as a Special Forces elite, he was being hunted by an enemy army in a violent war of attrition. Michael Ryan was an unemployed labourer who lived in the village of Hungerford over to the west. His father Alf had died aged 80 when Michael was 25. As an only child, Ryan was cosseted and doted upon by his mother, Dorothy, a former dinner lady at the local primary school, who, 12 years before, had taken up work as a part-time waitress in the Ramada Elcot Park Hotel in nearby Elcot. To Dorothy, Michael was her baby and the mother's only wish was for his happiness.

The squat, sullen, 27-year-old, who had been marked out as an underachiever at school, where he had been bullied and teased, received a succession of shiny motorcycles which transposed to new cars when he gained his driving licence. Ryan never retaliated against his school tormentors, instead becoming withdrawn and morose and a loner – the typical characteristics that run through every background of a civilian massacre. Michael Ryan was a ticking bomb waiting to explode. Nonetheless, he was an intelligent lad and a good worker, this testified to by local farmers, who often employed him as a casual labourer on their smallholdings.

The moment that Michael Ryan detonated came among the leafy summer foliage of the green Savernake Forest when he chanced upon the 'enemy'. This was Sue Godfrey, a 33-year-old diminutive – she was scarcely five feet tall – mother of two, who had chosen that Wednesday in August to drive from her home in Reading and picnic with her children in the woods. The children were excited; James was barely two and his sister Hannah was four.

Ryan was driving through the forest, following the main road that cut the forest in two, when he saw the small family group sitting around their blue groundsheet with the remains of the picnic spread before them. He pulled his grey Vauxhall Astra saloon into the side of the road not far from Sue Godfrey's black Nissan Micra. Whatever was going through Michael Ryan's warped mind as he watched the mum pack away her picnic debris and fold up the groundsheet will never be known. The children sat on the ground and watched the man's approach. He was carrying a large gun.

The gun was a Chinese manufactured 7.62 mm Kalashnikov assault rifle, one of the many firearms that he owned legitimately. Ryan's complete arsenal, kept in a Chubb metal gun safe in a shed in the garden of the house that he shared with his mother, included two 12-gauge shotguns, a Beretta semi-automatic 9 mm pistol, a .32 calibre pistol and an M1 .30 calibre carbine. On the day of the killings he carried the Beretta and the M1 in addition to the Kalashnikov.

Following the murders there would be much debate as to why a weapon such as the Kalashnikov would be licensed as a sports gun. The Kalashnikov is used extensively by terrorist militia and is the staple firearm of many Eastern Bloc armed forces. It is known as the 'widowmaker'. The debate would lead to a radical change in firearm laws in the UK, but such changes were in the future when Michael Ryan left his car and walked towards Sue Godfrey.

Mrs Godfrey, known to her family and associates as a cheery little person, would have greeted the man dressed in military camouflage with a smile – Savernake Forest was known for its survival enthusiasts and paintballers – but must have become alarmed when the taciturn Ryan ordered her to raise her hands and turn her back to him. He then marched her into the forest some 75 metres from the car. He also ordered her to take the groundsheet, which hints at the possibility of intended rape.

At some time between the order and the intervening minutes while Sue Godfrey begged for her life and that of her children, Ryan shot her 13 times in the back with the 9 mm Beretta, possibly as she attempted to escape, the heavy bullets smashing her to the forest floor and causing her children to scream in startled terror. Leaving the dead woman where she lay and ignoring the screaming children, Michael Ryan – feeling an unaccustomed wave of adrenaline and excitement wash over him – walked back to his car and drove off.

Ryan, living his dream of David Morell's *First Blood* – in which John Rambo, a returning Vietnam vet and the holder of the Congressional Medal of Honour, is bullied and ridiculed by a small-town police department until he takes on the army and the police force in a bloody slaughter – drove out of the forest and along the A4 towards Hungerford, pulling in to the Golden Arrow petrol station just before the town came into view. After filling a can with petrol Ryan approached the cashier's booth and fired the M1 through the glass at cashier Kakaub Dean. His first bullet missed and his fumbling fingers inadvertently hit the magazine release button causing the magazine to fall out before the second shot. Ryan ran back to his car and drove off. The attempt on the cashier's life had been witnessed by a motorcyclist, Ian George, who made an emergency call to the police to tell them a gunman was on the loose.

Now completely out of control and possibly enraged at his unsuccessful attempt to murder cashier Kakaub Dean, the perspiring Ryan arrived at his end terrace home at 4 South View, Hungerford, and promptly shot dead the family pet, a Labrador called Blackie. Throwing the petrol he had brought from the service station over the inert body of the dog, he torched the house. As the fire leapt to the adjoining properties he took the shotguns from his car and, answering the puzzled calls of neighbours, Roland and Sheila Mason, from their back garden at number 6, Ryan walked up the pathway between the two houses and shot them both dead at point-blank range. Roland Mason died under a hail of bullets from the Kalashnikov, and his screaming wife was dispatched with the Beretta.

Fully into his fantasy, the gunman now headed towards the town common, shooting and wounding local residents Marjorie Jackson and Lisa Mildenhall as he went. Wounded in both legs, 14-year-old Lisa Mildenhall narrowly escaped with her life. Overhead, a police helicopter tracked Ryan and local police set up roadblocks to stop traffic entering the town as they awaited the arrival of the police Armed Response Team. Ryan alternately switched from the Kalashnikov, to the M1 carbine, to the two shotguns that festooned his body. His fevered mind must have conjured up images of himself as John Rambo as he listened to the police and ambulance sirens that were the result of his shooting spree.

His next victim was Kenneth Clements, who was using

the same footpath approach to the common for a walk with his family, killed with a burst from the Kalashnikov. Ryan's aim was deadly, an instructor at the firing range where Ryan often practised with his weapons arsenal would later describe him as 'a damned good shot'.

Probably feeling too exposed on the common and aware of the surveillance helicopter overhead, Ryan turned and retraced his steps to South View, where his mother's home and three adjoining properties were burning, the local fire brigade unable to respond while Ryan prowled the town with his rifles and pistol. There, he was to have a fateful meeting with another victim.

PC Roger Brereton was a traffic officer on patrol in his police car when he heard the report of the shootings in South View. Although detailed to traffic duties and unarmed, PC Brereton turned his car in that direction and drove to intercept the gunman, his radio alive with messages of caution from the police control centre and warning of Ryan's indiscriminate firing against civilian targets. As the red, white and blue traffic patrol car turned into South View, Ryan struck a pose in the middle of the narrow road and emptied a nearly full magazine through the windscreen. Twenty-three bullets entered the car and PC Brereton was hit four times, one of the bullets passing through his neck and causing a fatal wound.

The police car zigzagged along the road before crashing into a telegraph pole as the dying officer managed to gasp out a radio message that he had been shot and requested assistance before he choked on blood and died. Unperturbed and still grinning insanely, Ryan turned his assault rifle on to a car driven by Linda Chapman who had just turned into South View with her daughter, Alison. Mrs Chapman was hit in the shoulder and her daughter sustained a wound in the upper thigh. Screeching to a stop at the sight of the grinning gunman dressed in combat gear, Mrs Chapman threw the car into reverse and roared back out of South View, managing to drive her car to the house of a doctor, where she crashed into a tree. Both women survived their wounds.

Not so fortunate was 84-year-old Abdur Khan who was working on his garden that bordered South View. Ryan casually shot him over the fence with the Kalashnikov and then fired at Alan Lepetit who was standing near an ambulance parked on the corner with the main Fairfield Road. Both the female ambulance attendant and Lepetit were slightly injured. As the ambulance drove hurriedly off, a car containing the husband of earlier wounding victim, Marjorie Jackson, turned into South View driven by Ivor Jackson's friend George White.

Marjorie Jackson had telephoned George White soon after her near escape from death at Ryan's hands and White had in turn called Marjorie's husband, but the reason the two men drove into South View is unclear. The quick-fingered Ryan killed George White and seriously injured Ivor Jackson, who feigned death after their vehicle crashed into PC Brereton's police car.

Amid all the confusion, Ryan's mother, Dorothy, who had been out shopping that fateful morning, turned her car into South View and surveyed the scene, aghast. George Jackson's car rested against the crumpled rear of a police car, the street was hazy with the mist and reek of cordite and her son stood in the road brandishing an assault rifle while behind him three homes, including her own, stood burning. This was her son, her little Michael, upon whom she doted. What had gone wrong while she shopped?

Dorothy Ryan climbed out of her car which she had parked behind George White's wrecked Toyota and approached her son, calling to him to 'stop his nonsense'. As if in a dream, Ryan turned towards her and pulled the trigger and Dorothy Ryan died amid a hail of bullets in the middle of the street where she had lived for 63 years.

The east end of South View narrowed into the footpath where Ryan had earlier shot and killed Kenneth Clements. The killer left South View by the path, skirting Mr Chapman's body, and turned south to cross the playing fields where he shot and wounded Betty Tolladay through the window of her home in Clarks Gardens. He then continued into Memorial Gardens where he met Frank Butler out walking his dog. With a smile in the man's direction, Ryan shot him dead.

At that point, for a reason that will never be known, Ryan discarded his much-loved M1 Underwood carbine and left the Memorial Gardens and shot and killed Marcus Barnard, a taxi driver, on his way to Bulpit Lane. Ryan was then seen to temporarily discard the Kalashnikov, possibly because it was empty, and return to pick it up and hang it over his shoulder. From that point on Ryan used the Beretta exclusively to kill his victims. There were certainly enough to choose from.

Due to a failure in communications and despite road-blocks being set up on the approaches to the town, people continued to move around Hungerford in cars and on foot. No police were available there to direct civilian traffic, the local force having withdrawn to the outskirts to await the arrival of the long overdue Armed Response Team. Proof of civilian movement came when Ryan shot and injured female motorist Ann Honeybone as she drove along Priory Avenue and John Storms, who sat in his stationary car in Ryan's path. Even the parents of a local police officer, who one would assume would be first on the 'warned' list, were shot as they drove their car along Fairview Road. Douglas Wainwright, father of PC Wainwright who had taken up station on the outskirts of town, was killed and his wife seriously injured. Kevin Lance, driving a Ford Transit van along Priory Avenue, received a minor flesh wound from Ryan's Beretta and Eric Vardy, driving a similar van in the opposite direction was shot and killed.

Another motorist, Sandra Hill, was killed as Ryan walked down Priory Road, where on impulse he broke into number 60, the home of Victor and Myrtle Gibbs. Once inside, the demented killer killed Mr Gibbs and seriously wounded Myrtle, who was later to die of her wounds in hospital. Leaving the house, Ryan shot at neighbours, injuring two more. At the same time the car containing Ian Playle and his family entered Priory Road from the south, having been denied entry via Park Street in the north-east because the armed and dangerous Ryan was believed to be in South View.

As the Playles' Ford Fiesta took the sharp, right-hand bend by Liguell Close, Ryan fired a snap shot at the driver, fatally wounding him. He was the last person to be killed by Michael Ryan. The last person injured would be George Noon of 109 Priory Road, who was shot on his back porch by Ryan as the gunman made his way to the rear of the

John O'Gaunt Community Technology College at the southern limits of the town. Mr Noon was shot at 1.45 pm. Police would later identify Ryan as present in the school building at 5.26 pm. His movements during the interim period are unknown and it has been speculated that he hid up in the school, where he had once been a pupil, during that time.

By 5.30 pm Michael Ryan had been contained within the school by a police cordon of armed officers. Although the gunman had been responsible for 16 deaths, including that of a police officer, and the wounding of 15 civilians, policy demands were that he must be given every chance to surrender himself and be given the services of a trained police mediator while holding the police at bay.

Ryan had positioned himself on the third floor, which gave an unrestricted view of the town. His presence in the school had been telephoned to the police by caretaker John Miles, a former Thames Valley policeman, whose children had seen Ryan's approach. The school was empty due to the summer holidays.

At 5.25 pm Ryan's Kalashnikov was thrown from the third storey. A few seconds later Ryan appeared at a window and remained there for one minute in full view of a police specialist sniper. The sniper did not fire. Sergeant Paul Brightwell, acting as mediator between Ryan and the police, finally opened a conversation with Ryan, warning him not to approach the windows with a weapon and assuring him that he would not be harmed if he surrendered himself. In turn, Ryan admitted that he had an Israeli fragmentation grenade and ammunition for the Beretta.

His conversation with Sgt Brightwell seemed to hang on

the condition of his mother – she was dead – and Ryan claimed shooting her was an accident. He also asked about his dog, the Labrador, Blackie. He explained to Brightwell that he had closed his eyes when he shot at the dog and thought perhaps he might have just winged it. Brightwell did not disclose that the dog or Ryan's mother were dead. 'Let them understand they have to come out to have their questions answered,' the police sergeant explained later, 'never give them closure on anything.'

The negotiations for Ryan's surrender seemed to have hit an impasse with his refusal to leave the building without news of his mother. Ryan also wanted to know the casualty figures, of which Brightwell pretended to be unaware, telling the gunman only that, 'You know you shot a lot of people.' To which Ryan replied: 'Hungerford must be in a bit of a mess,' and at one stage, self pityingly, 'It's like a bad dream – I wish I'd stayed in bed.'

The shouted conversation between police officer and gunman ended at 6.45 pm when Ryan again asked the time. All was then quiet until 6.52 pm when a muffled shot was heard from the third-floor classroom. Michael Ryan was dead, killed by single shot to the head from the 9 mm Beretta that had shattered his skull. He was the gun's ninth and final victim that day.

Footnote: The Hungerford rampage by Michael Ryan would see an abrupt change in Britain's gun laws. Shotguns held generally on a shotgun licence would have to be individually registered and magazines on semi-automatic and automatic models limited to a capacity for two shells only. Heavy calibre centre-fire rifles would be unavailable to the public without a special licence. On the horizon another tragedy was hovering which would almost totally remove the opportunity for the British public to own firearms. The tragedy of Dunblane was beckoning to British lawmakers.

CHAPTER 13

DEATH OF A HOSTESS

Tokyo, Japan, 1 July 2000

'I've got a lunch-date; I'll see you tonight'
— Lucie Blackman, to her roommate.

Lucie Blackman was a young woman who prided herself on her *chic* image. She wore her naturally blonde hair cut straight and falling across her finely chiselled profile and she walked as if she were on the concourse of a fashion show. Indeed, the tall, slim and elegant Lucie could have been a fashion model but instead she chose the less glamorous but more attainable position as a British Airways stewardess on long-haul flights to exotic worldwide destinations such as Japan.

Lucie loved Japan, especially Tokyo, with its shimmering nightlife and frantic bacchanalian lifestyle. So it was that in the spring of 2000 she left the airline to seek a new career as a hostess in the city's famed Roppongi district. On her previous breaks in Tokyo she had made connections and she arrived on 4 May, ready to start work. Even after the 13-

hour Virgin Atlantic flight from the UK she emerged from the aircraft looking crisp and smart. Travellers at the city's Narita Airport couldn't fail to notice the cool and sophisticated Westerner dressed in a silver-and-black ensemble that matched her Samsonite luggage as she strode towards the Arrivals Hall. Her expression was friendly but aloof, a look that carried a warning to male passengers that they could look all they wanted but touching was not on the agenda. Her cool blue eyes were hidden behind a pair of oversize sunglasses.

Lucie took a room in a *gaikokujin* hotel, an establishment that catered almost exclusively for foreigners and provided beds and soft pillows, in contrast to the wooden pillows and hard floors of the traditional boarding houses. Though homesick, she eventually found work in a hostess bar named Casablanca, a location no different from the scores of clubs in the district patronised by dollar-happy foreigners and Japanese businessmen who enjoyed the polyglot atmosphere of Americans in Brooks Brothers suits, svelte Russian models, pensioned-off rock stars, ingratiating local pimps and expressionless drug dealers, as well as the ever-present drunken US Marines of the homogenised former army of occupation.

Girls such as Lucie Blackman do not go to Roppongi contemplating a career in prostitution. There is a fine line between selling their bodies and selling their company as they sit at a guest's table encouraging him to buy the more expensive champagne and the finest cigar. They are not the girls of *consummation* where in some establishments even entertainers are expected to spend their free time between shows hustling the clientele and panhandling for drinks that are usually nothing more than coloured soda water sold at a disproportionate price, for which they notch up a commission.

Working in the clubs of Roppongi and pretending to be receptive to the schoolboy humour of inebriated Japanese clientele could be lucrative if the grateful client left a large tip at the end of the evening. The older sister of a friend in London had told Lucie of the opportunities open to an attractive young woman in the clubs of Roppongi.

No doubt Lucie, who had worked the rigid flight schedules of an airline stewardess, at first found the hours disorientating. Hostesses all over the world start work no earlier than 9.00 pm, and finish at around 2.00 am. As in most club-orientated industries, the tightly wound-up employees then go on to other clubs to unwind, often partying until dawn. The chosen venues in Tokyo in Lucie's time were the Gas Panic bar – a tongue-in-cheek reference to the Tokyo Metro 'Sarin Gas Attack' of 1995 – or the more salubrious establishments like the pricey Lexington Queen, where the continued presence of a well-heeled client and his wallet, both disinclined to call it a night, were always more than welcome.

Nonetheless, the life of a hostess in Tokyo wasn't the life of a lotus eater. The pressure to score was always on the girls who were paid strictly on results, and any girl who failed to add the expected number of arranged client dates, or *dohans*, to her tally each month would soon find herself unemployed and unemployable. The girls also worked illegally, since they had entered Japan on visitors' visas and had no work permits. This left them open to exploitation by their employers who were not above using a girl's status to bend a rebellious employee to their ways.

Just like every other young, attractive, blonde Caucasian

working in the hostess clubs of the Roppongi, Lucie got her share of offers to sleep with customers. The offers of money were simply staggering and the girls were free to do as they wished with no percentage going to the club, which carried on the legalised business of selling overpriced drinks to drunken clients and taking its 50 per cent *dohan* commission while avoiding any mention of overt prostitution. Lucie once told her mother in a telephone conversation that her job was to, 'Pour drinks, light cigarettes and discuss boring subjects like volcanoes.' She recalled that she often couldn't understand the English that her thick-accented customers insisted on speaking to her. 'I just nod,' she told her mother.

Lucie shared her *gaikokujin* hotel room with Louise Phillips, a friend who had travelled with her to Tokyo from England. Lucie told her family she was earning the equivalent of $1,500 a week and had struck up a relationship with an American named Scott Fraser, a young Marine stationed on the aircraft carrier *USS Kittyhawk*. Lucie last saw Scott Fraser on Friday 30 June, and told him she would be unable to keep a date for the next afternoon as she had arranged a *dohan* with a rich customer who had promised her a mobile phone if she would have lunch with him near the beach. These arrangements are common in Japanese club society, where a client, usually an older, prosperous businessman, will pay for the privilege of having an attractive hostess as a dinner guest and return her to the club in time for work. Lunch is a rather more personal matter, since most of the hostesses would prefer to sleep late. Nonetheless, Lucie made the effort and Louise Phillips recalls Lucie dressing for her lunch date in a black one-piece dress, matching thronged sandals, and a silver necklace with pendants in the shape of hearts.

Louise, Lucie, and Scott planned to meet up that evening and Louise received three calls from Lucie during that afternoon. The first was at 1.30 pm to say that she had met her lunch date; the second, at 5.00 pm, told Louise that everything was fine and that she was 'being taken to the sea'. The third was at 7.00 pm, shortly before Lucie had arranged to return to the hotel. She told her roommate she would be back in half an hour and phoned Scott with the same message, supposedly with her new mobile phone.

No one heard from her again but the next morning Louise Phillips received a strange phone call from a man who identified himself as Akira Takagi. Speaking in an accent so thick his English was barely intelligible, he told Phillips that Lucie was well and wanted her family to know that she was all right and had decided to join a spiritual cult. According to the mysterious caller Lucie was now training in Chiba, a large city on the eastern coast of Honshū Island. Louise Phillips passed the message on to Lucie's family who refused to believe their sophisticated daughter would choose such an alien lifestyle.

Lucie had never disclosed the name of her lunch partner and, as her usual homeward flow of daily e-mails and telephone calls ceased, her family back home in rural Sevenoaks in Kent became anxious and eventually flew out to Tokyo to launch a high profile media campaign in the search for their daughter. An anonymous businessman offered a reward of £100,000 and an information hotline was set up in Tokyo, staffed by expat residents. Although an arrest was made in October, the search and waiting continued throughout the year and Christmas came and went with no sign or word of Lucie Blackman. The blonde hostess appeared to have vanished into thin air.

Due to the massive publicity brought about by the efforts of the Blackman family, who even recruited the help of Virgin Airline boss Richard Branson to open a Tokyo office manned by expats, a hotline set up in the office soon began to get calls. Three foreign women told remarkably similar stories. They had all worked in the Roppongi district within the past few years and each had gone on a *dohan* date with a wealthy, well-turned-out Japanese businessman, who gave a different name, 'Kazu', 'Yuji', and 'Koji' on each occasion. Each woman reported blacking out and waking hours or days later in the man's apartment.

The search for Lucie Blackman was beginning to reach epic proportions, with her picture appearing on billboards and magazines all over Japan. The western media, ever alert for the opportunity of covert racism, published articles and essays on the Japanese male's moral approach to prostitution and the debasement of Caucasian women working in the murky world of hostess clubs and *dohan*-style assignments in Japan. More Tokyo Metropolitan police officers were assigned to the Lucie Blackman case than had worked on the 1995 'Sarin Gas Attack' in the subway system that had killed 12 and injured 5500. Their efforts bore fruit with an arrest on 12 October, when 48-year-old Joji Obara was detained as a suspect in an unconnected rape and questioned by detectives investigating Lucie's disappearance. Obara fitted the blueprint.

Joji Obara was a wealthy Japanese businessman, known to Tokyo police before Lucie's disappearance as a suspect in reported rape cases where increasingly popular date-rape drugs, such as the veterinary anaesthetic ketamine hydrochloride, were suspected of being used on the victims. When administered in small doses to humans, ketamine hydrochloride, known as Special K on the street, causes emotional detachment. The victim will suffer from a dissociative anaesthesia and is vaguely aware of, but comfortably detached from, all bodily sensations. Although the effect of the drug lasts less than three hours and can be detected in the body only up to 48 hours, in larger doses it can cause cardiac excitement, mild respiratory failure, coma and death. Obara had an apartment on Miura beach, a tiny windswept corner of the south side of Tokyo Bay, but subsequent searches of the area revealed nothing until February 2001.

The western side of Tokyo Bay is dotted with sailboat marinas, the rugged and rocky coastline considered ideal for the sport because of its steady offshore winds. The Miura coast is one such area favoured by families at weekends, where the Tokyo businessman can forget the smog of the city and take his brood to clear their lungs on the windswept coastline and enjoy the bracing sea air. On the Miura peninsula stands an apartment building called the Blue Sea. It is a white, four-storey block finished in stucco. Police had already searched Miura beach many times, considering it one of the areas where Lucie Blackman may have spent her lunch date 'by the sea'. To the right of the Blue Sea apartments a narrow drive leads down to the marina. To the left, a small path leads down to the tiny beach. Between two rocky clefts is a sandy area a couple of metres wide, a haven for beach detritus blown in by the wind. Years before, an eccentric bather, possibly acting on a whim, had hauled a bathtub to the cleft and installed it amongst the sand to enjoy a lazy saltwater bath in view of the sea yet sheltered from the strong winds that blew across Tokyo Bay.

Police had combed the area for four months, urged on by UK Foreign Secretary Robin Cook and Prime Minister Tony Blair, who had both mentioned the unresolved case during visits to Japan in the previous autumn. Now, on 9 February 2001, the police returned to Miura in an effort to discover whether Lucie Blackman had met her death on the mysterious lunch date with their main suspect Joji Obara, or had indeed left Tokyo as the mystery caller to Louise Phillips had indicated.

This time a police searcher poked around the sand at the base of the bathtub with a metre-long rod, which he sniffed after each probe. This search method, used by police and rescue squads over the world in searches for corpses, is a crude but effective procedure to locate decomposing organic matter below earth or snow, the unpleasant smell on the tip of the probe alerting the searcher to a possibly gruesome find. This time the search crew achieved a result. A dig down into the sand eventually revealed eight pieces of a decomposed torso, each wrapped in black plastic. The decay was so advanced that it was impossible to identify the gender of the victim. Police also recovered a block of cement that appeared to have been cast in the last six months and buried with the body parts. An X-ray revealed a human skull encased at the centre of the block.

Although suspicions were high that the recovered body

parts belonged to the vanished Lucie Blackman, DNA was not so advanced in Japan in 2001 and the condition of the body made identification difficult. Forensic officers therefore decided to break into the cement casing surrounding the head to check dental records against those of Lucie. As the cement crumbled, a gasp went through the examination room. A dental check, though demanded by procedure, would prove unnecessary, for spilling out of the cement casing were strands of long, natural blonde hair that had been shaved from the victim's head. Lucie Blackman had been found.

On 6 April, Obara, who maintained his innocence throughout, was charged with the murder of Lucie Blackman. Prosecutors suspected that her death had resulted from a rape that had gone wrong, and it was later revealed by unofficial police sources that Obara was suspected of being involved in as many as 200 rapes over a 25-year period. His arrest also closed the file on the murder of Australian Carita Ridgeway in 1992, for which, along with six other rapes, he was also indicted. The official assessment of Obara's rape record was based on the discovery of a private collection of 5000 home videos that included 200 showing Obara sexually assaulting unconscious women, demonstrating an obsession with the Japanese perversion of *yobai*, offered in certain, dedicated, sex shops known as 'image houses', where the client may pay and indulge his necrophilia obsession with prostitutes who feign sleep or death.

Joji Obara was born Kim Sung Jong in Osaka in 1952. His parents were Korean and his father was the wealthy owner of a string of *pachinko* parlours. Pachinko machines are a form of vertical pinball game devices in which the player launches a small metal ball which shoots upwards and then descends from pin to pin to either disappear into a hole and gain points or reach the bottom and oblivion. The game especially appeals to the Japanese notion of gambling by luck rather than skill and the elder Jong made a fortune. This allowed his son a prestigious education at Keio University.

He graduated with degrees in politics and law in 1981, and on the death of his father became a naturalised Japanese citizen, changing his Korean name to the more acceptable Japanese sounding one of Joji Obara. His career moves were less acceptable. While his mother retained control of the pachinko empire, her son moved into real estate and investment, narrowly escaping shame and disaster when his company collapsed with the Japanese economy in the late 1990s, when his mother bailed him out to the tune of many millions of dollars.

Following his arrest, a search of Obara's several apartments in Tokyo revealed a large variety of drugs, including chloroform and ketamine hydrochloride. An inclusion in a diary found by police was damning. In it Obara wrote, 'I cannot do a conscious woman.' Police also found blonde hairs that matched Lucie's and an undeveloped roll of 35 mm film that contained photographs of the missing woman posing for the camera. The problem in proceeding with the investigation was the absence of a body. Unperturbed and convinced they had their man, investigators built a case against Obara based on the evidence of victims traced from his collection of home videos and the statements of the three foreign hostesses who claimed they had been drugged at Obara's apartments. Joji Obara was remanded for trial on several counts of rape.

All the women interviewed recalled that once inside an apartment, Obara would offer them what he insisted was a rare imported herb wine. The wine invariably contained a drug that would render the victim unconscious. Ketamine hydrochloride, for example, had an effect of three hours but the videos clearly showed the diminutive Korean using a chloroform-soaked pad over their mouths. He would then commit the sexual abuse in a number of manners, including sodomising his victims while filming the assault using hi tech video equipment and lights.

Apart from the dangers implicit in an overdose of ketamine, police were aware that chloroform can have a toxic effect on the liver, causing death if administered continuously over a long period. Obara's excuse to his victims when they awoke unsteady and nauseous a day or two later was that they had taken too much alcohol or drugs and passed out.

Another murder was to be solved during the police investigation of their prime suspect in the Lucie Blackman disappearance when a researcher uncovered a hospital receipt that linked Obara to the hospital admission of a former Roppongi hostess, Carita Ridgeway, who had subsequently died of liver failure. The receipt revealed that in 1992 Obara had taken the gravely ill woman to Tokyo's Hideshima Hospital and told staff that she had fallen ill after eating bad shellfish. Due to what can only be described as a fortunate administrative fluke for investigators, Ridgeway's infected liver had actually been preserved at Tokyo Women's Hospital where the autopsy had been performed. Forensic pathologists now re-examined Ridgeway's liver and found toxic levels of chloroform. Obara was charged in connection with her death.

Another overlooked report emerged of Obara calling area hospitals late on the night of 2 July asking how to treat a victim of a drug overdose. A hardware store owner recalled Obara buying ready-mixed cement, a chainsaw, and other tools on 3 July. The house manager at Obara's Miura Beach apartment block also reported a tenant behaving suspiciously on the same day. Apparently, neighbours had complained about the noise of heavy machinery coming from Obara's apartment and he had refused to open the door. A police report filed that day by a patrol in the Miura beach area recorded that officers responding to the scene reported the tenant, Joji Obara, greeted them at the door with wet cement on his hands. The officers recalled that the tenant became agitated when they asked for permission to enter the apartment and refused to let them in. Assuming Obara to be an eccentric do-it-your-selfer, they left him with a warning to keep the noise down.

The Blackman family had been regular visitors to Tokyo following Lucie's disappearance. Sophie Blackman, Lucie's younger sister, had flown to Japan two days after her sister's reported disappearance and made regular trips between Tokyo and Sevenoaks throughout the investigation. Lucie's father, Tim, who was divorced from Lucie's mother, also joined the family search for his lost daughter, spending many thousands of pounds on family trips and accommodation. He was unconvinced, as were police, by a letter supposedly written by Lucie that arrived at police headquarters on 1 August. The letter read: 'I am doing what I want. Please leave me alone.' It was signed 'Lucie'.

Much criticism would surround Tim Blackman's acceptance of £450,000 *mimaikin*, or condolence money, from a business acquaintance of Joji Obara. The money was offered to the Blackman family following Obara's arrest. Payments were also offered and accepted by other victims and their families. Tim Blackman's ex-wife, Jane Steare, vilified the payment in the press, calling it 'blood money' but it cannot be denied that Tim Blackman had virtually bankrolled the family's presence in Japan. The prevailing feeling of both the defence and prosecution was that acceptance of the money signified a 'settling of the dispute' and would have an effect on sentencing.

However, the payment of *mimaikin* by Japanese perpetrators to their victims is not legally enforceable and is merely a gesture on the part of the accused to put him or her in a better light with the trial judge. This is at odds with the Sharia payment of *diyyah* paid under Moslem law as blood money to the family of a victim. The payment of *diyyah* represents the acceptance of the victim's family and the assailant or murderer that the matter is settled.

Whether the payment of *mimaikin* influenced the court, which is doubtful in the extreme, in April 2007 the Tokyo Lower Court found Obara guilty of nine rapes and of causing the death of Carita Ridgeway. He was acquitted of the rape and murder of Lucie Blackman due to the prosecution's inability to produce any forensic evidence that he had committed the crime. Joji Obara was sentenced to life imprisonment for nine rapes and the culpable homicide of Ridgeway. The verdict was greeted with disappointment by Blackman family sympathisers and much blame was directed at the Japanese police and judiciary whom, it was felt, had shown little interest in solving a case involving foreign women working illegally in Japan, many of whom, like Lucie Blackman and her friend Louise Phillips, had entered the country on a 90-day visitor's visa.

In an appeal lodged by the prosecution on 25 March 2008, Judge Hiroshi Kadono ruled that Obara had kidnapped Lucie Blackman on 1 July 2000, caused her death, and dismembered her body with a chainsaw. A further hearing by Tokyo High Court in December upheld the verdict. Obara's sentence of life imprisonment for Lucie Blackman's death will run concurrently with the sentence of the Lower Court.

CHAPTER 14

SLAUGHTER OF
THE INNOCENTS

Dunblane, Scotland, 13 March 1996
St Luke's Infants School, Wolverhampton, England,
8 July 1996

'He was swinging the machete at the kids and laughing'
— Ballbinder Bains, a witness to the machete
attack at St Luke's.

Thomas Hamilton was a 43-year-old bachelor with murder in his heart. He was a paedophile in the adulterated, modern sense of the word, who had indulged his perversities by becoming an assistant Scout leader, taking troops of boys up to the Scottish Highlands around Aviemore for overnight camping trips. His survival training inflicted on the immature boys was often extreme, imposing a Spartan regime that, one former troop member recalled many years later, often involved the boys bathing nude in cold mountain streams after which he would dry them with a towel, rubbing vigorously, and hugging them to his body to 'restore circulation'. Many of the boys returned home suffering from mild hypothermia, the result of the loss of body core temperature, and many parents complained to the local Scout leaders.

Their complaints eventually reached the headquarters of the Scotland Scouts Association and Hamilton was discreetly asked to stand down. Hamilton was incensed at what he saw as a slur on his leadership qualities and was angered that he would be barred from contact with his adolescent charges. He demanded an inquiry which was refused and he eventually had to tender his resignation.

Some of the speculation on Hamilton's motives for his subsequent horrific actions on 13 March 1996 suggested his hatred for children, but psychiatrists who have studied his actions point to a hatred of local society as his prime motivation. By killing the children, Hamilton was striking back at the roots of Dunblane, and his deadly spree was to leave a mark on the village that has yet to be erased.

Hamilton was born on 10 May 1952 in Glasgow Maternity Hospital, the issue of an already broken marriage. His parents, Thomas Watts and Agnes Hamilton, had been married only 18 months when Thomas left his pregnant wife for another woman. The couple had divorced by the time the baby Thomas, who would grow up to spread such misery, was born. The deserted Agnes gave the child her own surname and took a job as a hotel chambermaid to support herself and her baby. She eventually took Thomas to live with her adoptive parents in the east Glasgow suburb of Cranhill and the young Thomas grew up surrounded by a poorly considered family subterfuge of his grandparents' making, in which he became their natural son and his mother pretended to be his sister. He would be 22 years old before he would learn the truth.

In 1974, the family moved to Kent Road in Stirling, a few miles south of Dunblane on the A9. There the young Thomas attended the local school and worshipped regularly at the nearby Church of Christ. He also joined the local Boys' Brigade. His school years passed unremarked. He was remembered as a bright pupil, always near the top of his class in the term reports, and an enthusiastic member of the Brigade. He shunned girlfriends and began to develop an almost obsessive interest in firearms, buying magazines devoted to shooting and poring over the illustrations of shotguns, hunting rifles, and handguns. His vocabulary grew to contain names such as Webley, Colt, Beretta, and Browning.

In 1975 he successfully applied for a firearms licence and began collecting guns. He also became a member of several gun clubs in the area around Dunblane and Stirling where, like Michael Ryan in Hungerford, his dedication for practice would soon earn him the title of 'a good shot'.

Hamilton's questionable paedophile tendencies, although carefully disguised in his social life, soon led to an involvement with the Boy Scouts. In 1973 he was appointed Assistant Scout Leader of the Stirling troop, a title he bore proudly but would lose after the disastrous winter field trips. With time on his hands and his baser desires thwarted, Hamilton decided to open a chain of boys' clubs of his own, a project that would expose his darker character and serve to destroy his reputation within the community.

The venues were located in rented school gymnasiums,

public swimming baths, or church halls where Hamilton put the young club members – membership was open to boys aged from 7 to 11 only – through the Spartan routines that had cost him his leadership role with the Scouts. Some boys were cajoled into acts which made them feel uncomfortable and paid by Hamilton for their unwilling services. One of these recorded in police files refers to an episode where the nude Hamilton had boys smear him with suntan lotion all over his body while he writhed and groaned in ecstasy. The reason given to the boys for the exercise, which has never been revealed, must have been ingenious.

Complaints were sure to follow and Hamilton's clubs were put under police surveillance. His home in Kent Road, which he and his mother had inherited from his grandparents after their deaths, was found to be filled with photographs of half-nude young boys in various gymnastic positions, naked except for skimpy bathing trunks. However, police did not consider the photographs pornographic as defined by the law, since the boys had their genitals covered. This statement and other occasions when Hamilton appeared to be treated lightly by the police would be highlighted by the press after the events of 13 March 1996.

Rumours of Hamilton's depravity at his clubs grew and membership began to fall as concerned parents refused permission for their sons to attend, but the clubs – despite the occasional complaint of 'odd' behaviour – held a hidden attraction for members. Hamilton often took handguns and rifles on club field trips and taught the boys to shoot. Sometimes boys were camped on a deserted offshore island, left with a rifle and ammunition and the instruction to 'live off the land'. Boys reported that Hamilton would also attend to their scratches and insect bites by rubbing lotion onto parts of their bodies not always associated with their injuries. Word eventually reached the ears of Detective Sergeant Paul Hughes, then the head of Central Scotland Child Protection Unit. Hughes submitted a scathing report on Hamilton's activities and recommended that his firearms licence be revoked, citing Hamilton's 'unsavoury character and unstable personality'.

Hamilton continued to protest his innocence and wrote to various figures in authority, leading to later accusations in the wake of the Dunblane shootings that he was protected by his associates in high places.

Thomas Hamilton – bespectacled, balding, and with the countenance of Dickens's Mr Pickwick – was convinced that he was a victim of a conspiracy by police, a Scout movement angry at his success with the boys' clubs, teachers and parents. Psychiatrists would later gauge this as the time the hidden tide broke and he decided to take his ghastly revenge on the community. In the months before the school massacre he began to buy more guns and ammunition and became an even more regular figure at the local shooting ranges.

At 9.30 am on 13 March 1996, the chubby, perspiring Hamilton drove north-west along Doune Road and turned left into the lane that would lead him into the car park of Dunblane Primary School. There he parked his car and checked the pockets of the bulky haversack he carried across his shoulder. The haversack contained two Smith & Wesson .357 revolvers, two Browning 9 mm Hi Point semi-automatic pistols and 743 cartridges. The Brownings each carried a 14-round capacity magazine loaded with an alternating combination of full metal jacket armour-piercing and soft-nosed hollow-point ammunition. The full-metal-jacket round will pass through walls, doors, flesh and bone without distortion, while the lead hollow-point distorts on impact, flattening out to do massive damage to body organs and remaining within the body of the victim. Thomas Hamilton intended to inflict massive damage on his victims.

Having acquainted himself with the layout of the school from a boy who attended one of his clubs, the gunman first used pliers to cut telephone wires to the building then entered and made his way to the gymnasium, where a gym class of 16 five- and six-year-old pupils was in progress under the supervision of teacher Gwen Major. Hamilton entered the gym carrying both Brownings and proceeded to shoot down the diminutive pupils, killing or wounding 15 of the class including Gwen Major, who reacted as the gunman opened fire by throwing herself across a group of infants targeted by the killer.

Two other teachers in the gym were also hit as they tried to protect the children from the sudden hail of bullets. Blood spattered the walls as Gwen Major fell dead and small bodies were flung across the gym by the impact of 9 mm bullets smashing into vulnerable flesh. As the sound of gunfire resounded along the corridors of the school, a quick-thinking pupil on his way to class took refuge under a desk in the headmaster's office. The boy was eight-year-old Andy Murray, who would later find fame as a champion on the tennis courts of the world.

Pausing in the slaughter to change weapons, Hamilton

stepped out into the hallway and fired into other classrooms before opening fire through the walls of a mobile classroom. Inside the flimsy structure, children, alerted by their teacher, crouched under desks as bullets passed above them, snapping and buzzing through the air before burying themselves in books and cabinets.

The crazed gunman then returned to the gym to finish off the wounded. Fifteen children lay dead alongside their teacher and 17 wounded and traumatised survivors were still crawling for cover. Hamilton fired several more shots with the six-shot .357 revolvers then raised one to the roof of his mouth and blew his brains out, scattering a bloody pink mist upon the bodies of his victims. The massacre was over in minutes. Hamilton had fired 104 rounds and taken 17 victims with him to the grave.

Firemen and police were on the scene within 15 minutes and entered the charnel house of the blood-soaked gymnasium. Paramedics and police officers gave rudimentary treatment to the survivors while 11 children and three adults among the most severely wounded were rushed immediately to hospital, where one of the children was pronounced dead on arrival. The community was stunned by the sudden eruption of such lethal violence within its midst. Questions were asked concerning Hamilton's fitness to hold weapons and the local constabulary came in for much criticism, as did Hamilton's relationships with several authority figures in the community.

Thomas Hamilton was cremated in a private ceremony on 19 March, un-mourned by all except his elderly, shocked mother. A decision was taken by the school authorities to demolish the gymnasium and Dunblane Primary School underwent a refurbishment in an attempt to remove the stains of the massacre from human sight. The same could not be said of human consciousness, which still grieves in the small Scottish community.

The knee-jerk response to the Dunblane massacre moved swiftly to Parliament where MPs, urged on by a minority lobby, clamoured for greater gun control. A cynical administration, ever anxious to curb gun ownership in Britain, rushed through a series of measures that effectively limited ownership of handguns to .22 calibre, eroding that right with a second reading of the Gun Ownership Bill a few months later, a measure that closed down an area of legitimate sport for thousands of blameless enthusiasts, yet never questioned the inefficiency of the authorities that granted a firearms licence to an unstable pervert whose competency to own a gun had been questioned many times, long before the Dunblane incident.

Thomas Hamilton would not be easily forgotten, however. In Wolverhampton, that same year, a mental patient named Horret Irving Campbell was planning his own version of the Dunblane Massacre.

On Monday 8 July 1996, less than four months after Dunblane, a machete-wielding mental patient would run amok at a Blakenhall Wolverhampton primary school, inflicting hideous wounds on three adults and three infant pupils and almost severing the arm of a courageous young nursery assistant who went to their aid.

Panic had erupted at St Luke's Infants at around 3.30

pm that day when a man climbed over the school wall from an adjoining church plot and concealed himself among the perimeter bushes. An eyewitness described the man as black and of medium build but did not raise an alarm because he was, 'Just behaving like your average wacko and watching the kids – I thought he might have been collecting litter.' The group of 18 three- and four-year-olds were picnicking in the school grounds while attending the school with their care assistants to prepare them for joining the school as full-time pupils in the autumn term.

The man hiding in the bushes, keeping the children sitting on the grass under surveillance, was 32-year-old Horret Irving Campbell, a paranoid schizophrenic who had been released back into the community under a supervision order after receiving treatment in a mental hospital. Psychiatrists would later confirm that Campbell was fascinated by the Dunblane killer, Thomas Hamilton, and obviously planned to ape his actions. Campbell had not been able to obtain a handgun and instead he carried a 20-inch machete, or panga – a keen-edged weapon normally used for clearing undergrowth but lately favoured as a weapon of terror in the civil wars of Africa – as well as a knife and sponges impaled on metal rods that he later told police he intended to set alight and throw at children he had sprayed with petrol.

As the children cooed over the sticky buns on offer, a startled shriek greeted the appearance of Campbell who was running towards them waving the machete, laughing hysterically and shouting abuse. Three parents who attempted to block Campbell's mad rush towards the children were the first victims. These mothers – Surinder

Kaur, Azar Rasiq, and Wendy Wellington – all 29 years old, each received vicious slashing wounds. Lisa Potts, the 21-year-old nursery assistant who was to suffer such grave injuries protecting the children, reacted immediately. She leapt to her feet, grabbed a child under each arm and gathered others around her skirts before heading at speed for the school building.

She later recalled a blow across the back of her head then a hand in her hair pulling her backwards. She landed on her back but turned her body across the two children she was carrying while frantically grasping Campbell around the legs. As her charges fled she felt more felt heavy blows to her back, head and arms, and became aware of the man screaming at her in a language she didn't understand.

As the machete-wielding attacker vented his fury on the young nursery assistant, members of the school staff dragged the traumatised children – some of whom had been wounded in the madman's first dash across the grass – to safety. Four-year-olds Rhena Chopra and Francesca Quintyne both received deep cuts to their faces. Francesca suffered a deep slashing cut from her mouth to ear that broke her jaw and severed her ear. She would require many months of surgery, both reconstructive and plastic, to even partially repair the damage.

Ahmed Pervez, who was just about to celebrate his fourth birthday, was rushed to Birmingham Children's Hospital for emergency treatment to serious head and thigh wounds. Lisa Potts and the three parents who had suffered wounds coming to the children's aid were also detained in hospital, where their condition was described as stable. Miss Potts in particular had received massive lacerations to her back and hands as well as deep cuts to her head that exposed the skull in places. Her right arm had been almost severed in the attack and would leave her permanently disabled, with the grip in her right hand weakened.

In the confusion, Horret Campbell had disappeared, but he had been soon entering Villiers House, part of a tower block housing estate near the school. Police searched the building a number of times without success, returning on the Wednesday, two days after the attack, with dogs and finally located Campbell sitting on a stairwell on the ninth floor. A knife and a screwdriver were recovered from the scene. Campbell had lapsed into a deep depression and surrendered to police peacefully.

The case would be used to highlight the dangers of releasing mental patients back into the community and relying on supervision and the patient's medication to achieve normality. Police and media files contained many incidences of mentally ill patients attacking members of the public, often with fatal results for the victim, but NHS bean-counters refused to accept the danger and continued to urge the closure of institutions with the tacit agreement of the Home Office.

Denise Bennett, head teacher at St Lukes, paid tribute to staff members and parents who had risked their lives to protect the young and innocent victims. An unfeeling Criminal Compensations Board didn't react with equal compassion towards these unfortunates. Francesca Quintyne was awarded just £8100 for her injuries, later revised to £20,000, despite suffering persistent flashbacks and nightmares after the attack. She was represented at the Criminal Injuries Compensation Appeals Board by Cherie Booth QC. Lisa Potts, who was awarded the George Medal by HRH Queen Elizabeth II for her bravery during the attack, was eventually awarded £49,000 in compensation, which was raised to £68,300 on appeal. Miss Potts (now Mrs Webb, having married a policeman) has gone on to write several self-help books for children. She also founded the Christian charity 'Believe to Achieve', aimed at encouraging independence and enhancing self-esteem in children.

At his trial at Stafford County Court on 9 December 1996, Horret Irving Campbell claimed he had been seeking revenge against St Luke's infant pupils whom, he insisted, ran to the school fence and hissed racial remarks at him whenever he passed by the school. He told the court he was obsessed by Thomas Hamilton, whom he believed had been victimised, and wished to imitate the carnage of Dunblane. He also accused the children of St Luke's of conspiring to poison him. He was found guilty on seven counts of attempted murder and sent to high security Ashworth Hospital in Liverpool for 12 weeks' assessment before sentencing, and was diagnosed as suffering from auditory hallucinations resulting from extreme paranoid schizophrenia. In March 1997 Campbell was ordered by the presiding Justice Sedley to serve indeterminate detention in a secure mental institution.

In July 2009, St Luke's Infant School and the Primary wing were demolished and a new £6.5 million replacement school built in nearby Park Street South. Three years earlier, Villiers House and the accompanying three tower blocks that made up the infamous Blakenhall Gardens estate were also demolished, removing the visual memories of a tragedy that nonetheless will always remain in the minds of those who witnessed the madness of Horret Campbell and heard the terrified shrieks of his victims.

CHAPTER 15

FROM RUSSIA WITH EXTREME PREJUDICE

London W1, England, 1 November 2006

'You have shown yourself to have no respect for life, liberty or any civilised value'
— Alexander Litvinenko, in a letter to Vladimir Putin.

The victim of this piece, Alexander Valterovich Litvinenko, was born in Voronezh, Russia, then part of the USSR, on 30 August 1962. He was the son of a doctor, Valter Litvinenko, and enjoyed the comparatively middle class upbringing and education usually provided by those of his father's calling. At 18 he left school and was drafted into the Soviet Army. The young Alexander felt immediately at home in the military and from a humble private moved rapidly up through the ranks to lieutenant colonel. From there, in 1988 at the age of 26, the state-groomed Lt Col Litvinenko joined the Soviets' feared intelligence wing, the Komitet Gosudarstvennoy Bezopasnosti (KGB) where he worked in counter intelligence. Showing his mettle in combating the state's enemies, he eventually moved on to work in collaboration with the Moscow Police, in a special unit that had been established primarily to combat rising organised crime within the capital.

On 19 August 1991 communist hardliners led by former vice-president Gennady Yanayev staged a coup that ousted the increasingly liberal Soviet president, Mikhail Gorbachev. These were dark days in the new Russia. As Gorbachev was confined to his dacha in the Crimea, within the KGB the old guard manoeuvred for position and power. Outside on the streets tanks patrolled the square outside the Russian Parliament, and Yanayev appeared on television flanked by the heads of the army, police, and KGB, to insist the combined force had averted a national disaster. The Russian people thought otherwise and came out in force to protest against the takeover. Their leader was the president of the newly formed Russian Federation, Boris Yeltsin.

Yeltsin, in a rare sober moment, climbed onto a tank to confront the army and appeal to the troops not to turn against the people. The people followed Yeltsin in his call for civil resistance and, with the army behind him, defeated the coup – a defeat that featured a spectacular tank attack on the Duma and brought about the break-up of the Soviet Union.

The KGB was also disbanded, shedding its dark image to become the more gently named Federal Security Service (though carrying on its counter-intelligence operations under the wing of the FSB Section 1) and Lt Col Litvinenko was appointed deputy head of the slightly more benign Section 7, in charge of Internal Affairs to investigate corruption within. It was during this time that

Boris Berezovsky, Secretary of the Security Council and a close associate of Boris Yeltsin, was marked for assassination, according to Litvinenko in his later days of disillusionment, by order of old communist hands within FSB Section 1. Berezovsky promptly fled to London.

It may have been at that time that the young lieutenant colonel began to fall out of love with the Socialist dream, but if so there should have been pause to look over his shoulder. Steadily climbing through the ranks to eventually take control of the FSB was a sinister figure that would play an essential role in Litvinenko's future career. The man, destined to become the head of FSB and later president of the Russian Federation, was Vladimir Vladimirovich Putin.

Twelve years Litvinenko's senior in age, Putin was a rising star whose meteoric rush would see him become the second president of Russia after Boris Yeltsin and prime minister and principal string-puller in the government of Dmitry Medvedev when his second term of presidency ended in May 2008.

In 1998 Putin was established as head of the FSB and it was at this time that Litvinenko inadvisably went public with his version of the plot to murder the self-exiled Berezovsky. He was dismissed from his post at the FSB and promptly arrested and charged with abusing his office, for which he spent nine months in Lubijanka Prison. In 2000 another warrant was issued for his arrest after statements attributed to him appeared in the Western press. He was charged with giving false evidence relevant to an investigation and fled to Turkey before he could be sent back to the Lubijanka. He was joined in Turkey by his wife Mariana and their son Anatoly, who had managed to flee Russia on tourist visas.

In November 2000 Litvinenko and his family gained entry to Britain, where he successfully applied for political asylum. There, under the protective umbrella of the UK's homeland intelligence MI5, he settled with his family in Kensington, West London, but moved out after Mariana Litvinenko reported being bothered by sightings of 'large men in poorly-cut suits' near their home. The family was transferred by MI5 to Muswell Hill in North London where Litvinenko, no doubt indulging himself in a sense of false security, launched a vitriolic campaign of criticism against the newly elected President Putin and his policy towards Chechnya.

Throughout their stay in London, Litvinenko and his family were supported by Boris Berezovsky, the Russian oligarch and multi-millionaire who had fled to Britain when Litvinenko exposed the plot on his life in 1998. It was Berezovsky who flew 50 journalists in from Moscow for a Whitehall press conference in 2002, when Litvinenko authored a book *Blowing Up Russia – Terror from Within*. In the book Litvinenko alleged that Russia was behind the 1999 apartment bombings in the cities of Buynaksk, Moscow and Volgodonsk that killed 300 people and had been blamed by Putin on Chechen separatists. Three years later Litvinenko claimed in a Polish newspaper that he had proof that in 1998, al-Qaeda key figures had received training from Russian Federal Security operatives in Dagestan. Litvinenko was fast gaining a reputation as a vehement critic of Putin and Russia, and UK intelligence services could only advise caution and warn him that the arm of Russia was long.

Above: Lucie Blackman (*left*), 21, was working as a hostess in Japan when she was murdered by Joji Obara (*right*) in July, 2000.

Below: Lucie's father, Tim Blackman, speaks to the Japanese press after visiting the cave where his daughter's dismembered body was discovered in January, 2001.

Above left: America's worst serial killer, 'Green River Killer' Gary Ridgway, in court in November, 2003. He murdered at least 48 women during the 1980s and 90s.

Above right: Family members react as Ridgway pleas guilty in court.

Below: Over 900 members of Peoples Temple, an American cult led by Jim Jones, died in Guyana in 1978. Until the events of 9/11, it was the largest single loss of American civilian life in a non-natural disaster.

Above: On 3rd October, 2002, 54-year-old part-time taxi driver Premkumar Walekar was shot and killed at a petrol station in Aspen Hill. He was one of the first victims of the Washington sniper.

Below left: 17-year-old John Lee Malvo, one of the snipers, pictured leaving court in Virginia in December, 2002. He was sentenced to six consecutive life sentences without the possibility of parole.

Below right: The other sniper, Gulf War veteran John Allen Muhammad, was executed by lethal injection in November, 2009.

The second plane hits the World Trade Center on the most infamous date in modern history: September 11th, 2001.

The aftermath of the devastating Oklahoma City Bombing in 1995,
which claimed 168 lives. Timothy McVeigh (*inset*) was later convicted
of the attack. He was executed in 2001.

In the image: CAMERA 14 · 07:21:54 07/07/05 · ítv news · **BREAKING NEWS** POLICE CHIEF: CONCERNED THIS WAS A CO-ORDINATED ATTACK · 11.59 Jul 07 LONDONERS: REMAIN WHERE YOU ARE. DO NOT TRAVEL

Above: A CCTV image of the four suicide bombers as they arrive at Luton Train Station on their way to London on 7th July, 2005.

Below: The world was in shock as news of the bombings broke.

As an intelligent man, Alexander Litvinenko was aware that his public criticism of Putin and his regime placed him in mortal danger. On advice from MI5 his London address was kept secret and his e-mail and telephone number were constantly being changed. He also refused to see anyone in private, always insisting on meeting in public places. He was also aware that Moscow wanted him back. Two years after his arrival in Britain he had received a letter ordering him back to Moscow to face charges of corruption in office. He explained the charges in a public statement: '*I was given illegal orders linked to the kidnapping and murder of people. When we did not execute these orders, they began to persecute us. Criminal cases against me were opened. I was offered a higher post in exchange for my silence. I have written 15 reports detailing these abuses, which are with me in Britain.*' Litvinenko was eventually sentenced in his absence by a Moscow court to three-and-a-half years' imprisonment.

In October 2006 Litvinenko took the floor at a meeting of the Frontline Club, a London meeting place for journalists, and denounced the Russian government for the murder of Russian journalist and human rights activist Anna Politkovskaya, who had been a constant critic of Putin and his dealings in Chechnya. Politkovskaya was shot and killed as she exited the elevator in her Moscow apartment building on 7 October 2006. It was this announcement that possibly rattled the corridors of power in the Kremlin, and those corridors all led to the office of one man who now occupied the seat of power – President Vladimir Putin.

Twelve days later, on 1 November, Litvinenko had an arranged meeting with an Italian acquaintance at the Itsu sushi restaurant in Wardour Street, Piccadilly. Mario Scaramella later recalled that the discussion over lunch concerned Litvinenko's assertion that Italian ex-prime minister Romano Prodi was connected to the FSB. Scaramella, who was working for the Mitrokhin Commission investigating FSB penetration of Italian politics, in turn had offered information on the death of journalist Anna Politkovskaya. Scaramella is a mysterious figure in the story surrounding the murder of Alexander Litvinenko. A Neapolitan by birth, he described himself as an academic, although none of the universities he claimed to have attended seemed to acknowledge him.

Later that day Litvinenko met with two former FSB officers, Andrey Lugovoi and Dimitri Kovtun. After the meeting he returned home and that evening ate dinner with his wife Mariana. Later he began to develop stomach pains and vomiting. The next day the pain was so severe and the bouts of vomiting so regular and intense that he was hospitalised in University College Hospital in central London.

Litvinenko's condition immediately raised the suspicions of MI5 and intensive tests were made for known poisons, during which his condition deteriorated rapidly. Radiation poisoning was suspected due to the rapid failure of bodily functions and hair loss, but first tests were for thallium, after the presence of gamma rays proved negative. This was because Litvinenko had been poisoned with polonium-210, a radioactive isotope probably chosen because it does not emit gamma rays, which are easily picked up by hospital equipment. Polonium emits only alpha particles which are invisible to normally employed radiation detectors. It was only in the final hours of his life that Litvinenko was tested for alpha-emitters, an examination that requires special and extremely sensitive equipment. But it was not until after death and during autopsy that the deadly concentration of polonium-210 was detected in his body.

The discovery of such a potent source of radiation caused consternation among investigators, who now had to trace a trail of potentially lethal radiation across London. Litvinenko had been killed by a dose equivalent to 10 micrograms of polonium-210 – 200 times the average lethal dose for a human – administered at one of the locations he had been at on 1 November. These locations would be dangerously infected with radiation, as would the vehicles he had travelled in that day. Members of the public with whom he had come into contact would have to be tested for lethal levels. The search teams sprang into action across London. Help was requested from the US Federal Bureau of Investigation and its specialist experts on counter radioactive warfare.

Only two distinct polonium trails were traced across London, left by the Russians Lugovoi and Kovtun, and Litvinenko. Reports circulated at the time by a journalist friend of Mario Scaramella claimed the Italian showed five times the acceptable level of radiation. These were afterwards proved false. The drama was further enhanced by the news that Scaramella disappeared shortly after Litvinenko's death and was rumoured to be in hiding in fear of his life. Traces of polonium-210 were found in various London bars and restaurants and in a vehicle owned by a Lambeth taxi company. These were never explained fully by the investigation and could relate to establishments visited by someone carrying the radioactive polonium isotope.

Detectives finally decided that Litvinenko had been poisoned on the afternoon of 1 November at the Millennium Hotel in Grosvenor Square, West London. The time set was 5.00 pm – strangely at odds with the levels at first reportedly found on Scaramella and at Itsu, the sushi restaurant where the two had eaten lunch. Investigators based the time on an examination of the bus on which he had travelled to the hotel. The bus was found to be free of radiation whereas large amounts were detected in a room in the hotel and in a teacup in the hotel's Pine Bar.

Radiation was also found at Berezovsky's office where Litvinenko had stopped on his way home to use a fax machine, and in the radio car taxi that picked him up from Berezovsky's office to take him to his home in Muswell Hill. Items that he had touched at home were also contaminated, because polonium-210 is secreted through the pores onto the skin rather than contaminating by proximity. Mariana Litvinenko tested positive for radiation but here a strange fact emerged. Litvinenko's wife left no secondary trail passed on to Anatoly or the things she touched, allowing investigators to assume that anyone who left a trail must have been in direct contact with the material.

While this might have pointed to Scaramella, whose level of contamination and that of the Itsu on 1 November was never officially confirmed, it was a definite pointer to the Russians, who would have became contaminated simply by opening the radioactive container of polonium-210. What is clear is that when Litvinenko boarded the bus at 5.00 pm that took him to Grosvenor Square, he had had no direct contact with the material that would eventually kill him and therefore left no trail on the vehicle. When he left the hotel where he had made contact with the Russians he was figuratively glowing like Chernobyl. So high was his level of contamination that the family home was classified as uninhabitable and the car that had brought him home to Muswell Hill had to be destroyed.

It was established that Lugovoi and Kovtun had previously had an earlier meeting with Litvinenko at the Millennium on 16 October. It was also noted through contamination levels that a similar contact had occurred at the Itsu restaurant at a different table on or about that date. Since the Itsu was a favourite eating place on Litvinenko's London circuit, and where he would customarily choose to meet people for lunch, it can be assumed that the Russians had either met him on those previous occasions to rehearse the poisoning or the attempt had been unsuccessful.

Investigators were able to differentiate between the trails left by Litvinenko and the Russians because they left a stronger trail than their target. Once ingested, polonium is secreted through the skin in small quantities, whereas traces passed on from direct contact would give a much stronger signal.

Alexander Litvinenko died on 23 November at the age of 43 after lingering an agonising three weeks as the polonium radiation destroyed his internal organs. His wife Mariana recalled their last conversation, which took place on the previous evening as she left her husband's bedside to go home to their son. 'He couldn't move, he was paralysed, but he managed to whisper to me, *"Mariana, I love you so much"*. I told him I had not heard this for a long time and it made me happy. It was the last words he spoke to me.'

Although not a practising Muslim, Litvinenko had made many Muslim friends due to his determined defence of Chechen separatists. On 7 December a funeral reading took place at the Central London Mosque after which his lead-lined coffin was taken to Highgate Cemetery for burial. Three days after his death, the *Mail on Sunday* published a statement on its website attributed to Litvinenko in which he addressed himself to the Russian president:

'This may be the time to say one or two things to the person responsible for my present condition. You may succeed in silencing me but that silence comes at a price. You have shown yourself to be as barbaric and ruthless as your most hostile critics have claimed. You have shown yourself to have no respect for life, liberty or any civilised value. You have shown yourself to be unworthy of your office, to be unworthy of the trust of civilised men and women. You may succeed in silencing one man but the howl of protest from around the world will reverberate, Mr Putin, in your ears for the rest of your life. May God forgive you for what you have done, not only to me but to beloved Russia and its people.'

Scotland Yard's Anti Terrorism Unit continued its investigation, focusing on the movements of Lugovoi and Kovtun. Strong radiation traces were found from Lugovoi's visit to the office of Boris Berezovsky the day before the former's final meeting with Litvinenko. Kovtun had also left traces in Hamburg Airport's transit lounge during a flight from Moscow to London in the days before the meeting at the Millennium Hotel. Polonium-210 radiation was also found in four British Airways aircraft that had carried the Russian duo back and forth. While investigators implicated neither of the two Russians in Litvinenko's death, Andrey Lugovoi was later the subject of a Scotland Yard extradition request for questioning that was refused by Moscow. The threat of massive radiation sickness among the UK population was heightened by Lugovoi's revelation that he had attended the football match between Arsenal and CSKA Moscow on 1 November. British Airways presented the UK Health Protection Authority with a list of flights by the radiation infected aircraft that involved over 30,000 passengers. Stringent efforts were put into effect to find anyone who might have been in contact with either of the Russians during their time in the UK and no one tested showed more than a minimal trace of radiation. Polonium-210 has a half-life of 140 days.

The involvement of Lugovoi and Kovtun in Litvinenko's death was stringently denied by Moscow but a new light was shed on Russian involvement when scientists at the Atomic Weapons Research Establishment traced the source of the polonium to a nuclear power plant in Russia. In May 2007 the British Foreign Office submitted a request to Moscow for the extradition of Andrey Lugovoi to the UK to face criminal charges relating to Litvinenko's murder. The request was refused.

Speaking on NBC News two months later, Russian expert and security consultant Paul Joyal said: 'A message has been communicated to anyone who wants to speak out against the Kremlin: "*If you do, no matter who you are, where you are, we will find you and will silence you – in the most horrible way possible*".'

CHAPTER 16

THE MURDER AND RAPE OF CAROLINE DICKINSON

Pleine-Fougères, France, 18 July 1996

'I thought she was having a nightmare'
– Caroline's dormitory mate, Ann Jasper.

End-of-term school trips are a fun tradition among schoolchildren. With the term over, pupils can look forward to a long holiday without homework and an opportunity to join their classmates on a trip abroad with their teachers. Parents often happily contribute to the cost, sure that their offspring will be in safe hands, and the children themselves become involved in raffles and ruses to raise money.

Such a trip was planned for the pupils of Launceston Community College in Cornwall as the summer term of 1996 drew to a close. Their destination would be Brittany in France for an opportunity to brush up on the language and do some sightseeing. The impending trip was greeted with much excitement by the party of 40 pupils who would participate, overseen by five teachers. A ratio of one teacher to eight pupils seemed reasonable to parents; the children would be well taken care of. But as the ferry left the Poole harbour breakwater en route to St Malo and was picked up by the gentle summertime roll of the English Channel, one pupil was taking her last glimpse of England's chalk-white southern cliffs.

For 13-year-old Caroline Dickinson, from Bodmin, was destined by fate to return to the shores of her homeland in a coffin after death had sought her out in a small Brittany village. Caroline would never see her family again and the world would recoil with horror at the depravity of the crime.

The school party of 35 girls and five boys had left Launceston by coach for the journey to Poole. On arrival in St Malo they had re-boarded the coach for the drive to the youth hostel they would be staying at – the Hostal Mont St Michel in Pleine Fougères On the way, the children would stop for the opportunity to see something of St Malo, the famous mediaeval tapestry of Bayeux, and the majestic Mont St Michel. They'd also have a chance to sample French cuisine, no doubt accompanied by jokes about frogs' legs and snails, and try out their knowledge of French on the natives.

Thursday 18 July turned out to be very hot and the day's activities had left most of the schoolchildren exhausted and ready for bed after supper. Caroline had especially asked to share a four-bunk dormitory with her friends, Ann Jasper and Melissa Hutchings, along with two other girls, and a mattress had been provided to allow her to sleep at floor level between the two bottom bunks. Excited by the adventures of the day and the trip, which was the first Caroline had spent away from her parents, John and Sue Dickinson, and her 11-year-old year old sister Jenny, Caroline sat on her mattress in her pyjamas singing along with her roommates. Complaints from other rooms soon caused a teacher to knock on the door at midnight and order them to sleep, and the five girls spent an hour-and-a-half whispering to each other before sleep finally overtook them all.

Sometime during the night, Ann Jasper, on a top bunk, was awakened by the sound of Caroline calling for her mother and begging for help. The sound of Caroline's voice was accompanied by the sound of muted thrashing and Ann assumed her friend was having a nightmare. The sound soon stopped and Ann drifted back to asleep. Melissa Hutchings, who was on a bottom bunk on a level with Caroline's mattress, awoke to the sound of banging, then a sleeping bag zip being pulled down and thought she saw a figure standing in the room. She assumed it was Caroline on a trip to the loo in the passage outside the small dormitory.

At 8.00 am the next morning a knock on the door indicated that it was time to get up and wash before breakfast, but Caroline appeared to be sleeping on. Calls by her roommates got no response, so Melissa Hutchings playfully took matters into her own hands and tipped the mattress over. The sleeping bag was unzipped and gaping open. Melissa noticed her friend was wearing no pyjama bottoms. Caroline could not be roused and her lips and face were blue. She also felt cold to the touch. The worried girls immediately alerted a teacher who, after a brief examination of the apparently unconscious Caroline, ordered them from the room.

After frantic attempts by teachers to revive the seemingly unconscious girl, police and an ambulance were called but Caroline Dickinson was beyond help. She had been suffocated by a wad of cotton wool being stuffed into her mouth, the residue of which was still evident on her lips and chin, and she had clearly been raped. Fifty gendarmes were immediately assigned to the case as the shocking news broke on TV, radio and newspapers on both sides of the Channel: a 13-year-old schoolgirl had been raped and suffocated to death while on a school trip to France. The news alarmed parents everywhere.

John and Sue Dickinson flew immediately to Brittany; it was to be the first of 18 trips John Dickinson would make to appeal to the French public for help to find his daughter's murderer. The French police moved rapidly, arresting a homeless vagrant 65 kilometres from Pleine Fougères on suspicion of Caroline's murder. The suspect, Patrice Pade, a man in his forties with a long history of rape and violence towards women, obligingly confessed to the murder, and examining magistrate Gerard Zaug thought he had his man, but traces of semen found on Caroline's body did not match DNA samples given by Pade and he was released on 7 August with the investigation now back to square one.

Another suspect who bore a striking resemblance to a photofit of the killer, drawn from information by eyewitnesses who had noticed a stranger lurking near the hostel, had fled his home in August with his two children after killing his wife. Dr Yves Godard was seen on the Isle of Man in September and became the new focus of Magistrate Zaug's search for a killer. Dr Godard, who is still sought by French police for the murder of his wife, is now the subject of an international arrest warrant. Eventually Zaug was removed from his position after criticism from the UK press and Caroline's parents, who felt that the magistrate's wild-goose chases were born out of desperation and were allowing the real killer to go free. Truer words were never spoken, for it would transpire that Caroline's killer was already far beyond the reach of French justice.

An examination of the contents of Caroline's stomach during the autopsy showed her evening meal to have been fully digested, and placed the time of her death at around 3.30 am. Unseen at that early hour, a British registered Renault 5 driven by the killer had left the area and by that same afternoon would be parked in a side road in Earl's Court, West London, while its owner avidly devoured the news of the rape and murder of the schoolgirl in Brittany and relived the ecstasy of the killing.

Caroline's killer, Francisco Arce Montes, born in Gijón, northern Spain, in March 1950, was a loner with few friends, who often spoke of his miserable childhood. His mother, possibly sensing the monster she had brought into the world, despised her son. Mental problems developed in his early teens when he developed an obsessive personality, refusing to eat unless his food was arranged in a certain manner on his plate and insisting on washing his hands in mineral water before eating. By the age of 20 he developed sexual aberrations and a desire to expose himself to a young female neighbour. He was arrested and diagnosed with chronic paedophile tendencies towards young girls and paranoid schizophrenia.

The murder of Caroline Dickinson formed part of a long established pattern where he would tour Europe seeking out young girls at youth hostels and then sneaking in at night to rape. He once told a friend, 'I like them young, between 11 and 12. After 20, I lose interest.' Montes had picked Caroline out of her group earlier on the day of the murder when he saw her in the square at Mont St Michel. Excited at the prospect of sex with such a young and pretty child, Montes had followed the coach back to Pleine Fougères and noted that the party was staying at the town's youth hostel. The fantasy ended when he suddenly recalled his forgotten original intention to return to England following some near scrapes with the gendarmerie when he had nearly been caught stalking schoolchildren earlier that week. Turning the car around, he headed for St Malo and the ferry to Portsmouth but arrived too late for the last crossing. Caroline Dickinson's fate had been sealed by a maritime timetable.

Montes then decided to drive to St Lunaire, just west of St Malo. Depressed at missing the ferry he drank heavily in the local bars and returned to his car to pop some pills and sleep – but the thought of the pretty young girl in the square at Mont St Michel would not let him rest and he lay awake until the urge forced him to look for prey at the nearest youth hostel.

St Lunaire youth hostel, like many in the Brittany area, is in a remote location away from the town but near enough to the local sightseeing attractions. Relishing the darkness and solitude of the location, Montes waited until after midnight before entering the hostel at the rear where, as ever, he found a door unlocked.

Minutes later, 13-year-old Kate Wrigley, who was due to return the next day from her school trip to France, felt her underclothes pulled from her body and a pad clamped across her mouth and nose. The pad stung and burned her face and she kicked out at the partition that separated her from the bed of her friend Jenna Ellis close by. Jenna raised herself up to look over the partition wall and saw a man half-kneeling above her friend. She shouted and the man rose from Kate Wrigley's bed and calmly walked out of the room.

Leaving the shouting behind him, Montes returned to his car in an angry mood. He had so nearly had the girl in his grasp and someone had intervened. His sexual intensity was at such a height that he would not rest until he had found relief. He remembered the school party he had followed to Pleine Fougères earlier that day. He started the Renault 5 and drove south-east. It was 2.30 am and in an upstairs room of the Hostal Mont St Michel, Caroline Dickinson was already settling down for the night that was to be her last on earth.

Arriving at the hostel still groggy from drink and drugs, Montes parked the dust-covered Renault at some distance and reconnoitred the main building on foot. The hostel was contained in a two-storey farmhouse with a dormer window and skylights in the tiled roof with a four-pot chimney at each gable end. The windows of both storeys had exterior wooden shutters which seemed to be fixed permanently open, more for decoration than security, although he didn't doubt they could be fastened from inside in an emergency.

Outhouses led off from the main house, including a single-storey extension to the left that he assumed would be a dining room.

The dormitories in which the children slept would almost certainly be upstairs. The buildings were all but shielded from the road by trees which, although not giving him perfect cover, provided areas of shadow in which to move. Two separate glass-framed doors stood between shutters on the right of the two downstairs windows. Slipping close to the wall, he pushed the nearest frame and heard the click as the door opened and swung inwards. His sexual excitement almost overwhelmed him as he moved silently towards the stairs.

The steps creaked alarmingly and he spread his feet to place his weight near the wall. His brain was still fogged with the effect of the alcohol and drugs but the thought of release and the feel of a young, firm body under him heightened his arousal until he found it difficult to breathe. At the top of the stairs a line of doors extended away, some closed, some ajar.

Outside the door of Number Four he paused at the sound of deep, measured breathing that told him the occupants were asleep. He eased the door inwards and it stopped against something on the floor before it reached the full 90 degrees. He looked down and saw a mattress and the foot of what appeared to be an occupied sleeping bag. He slipped into the room and closed the door quietly behind him.

A few hours earlier, in the aborted attack on Kate Wrigley in St Lunaire, Montes had used a swab of alcohol to disorientate his victim. Although the type of alcohol has never been identified by police, a liquid strong enough to burn on contact with the skin – Kate Wrigley and other victims had complained of a burning sensation around their nose and mouth – would almost certainly have been rectified spirit, a highly volatile mixture of 95.6 per cent ethanol and water, used in the production of liqueurs or for mixing with cordials to give a mind-bending punch. Sudden inhalation of the vapour would certainly be enough to render a person temporarily confused and unable to react. This night, however, Montes had not prepared himself fully for a new attack and carried only the cotton wool swab he had used at St Lunaire, from which most of the alcohol had evaporated.

Kneeling down on the floor by the mattress he was aware of sleeping figures in bunks either side of him but the proximity of possible discovery always excited Montes further. Quietly, listening to his own frantic heartbeat, he pulled down the zip of the sleeping bag and revealed the form of the sleeping girl. Someone stirred on a bunk above him as he unzipped his trousers and leaned forward to clamp the cotton swab across the girl's mouth and tug at her pyjama bottoms. His young victim kicked and struggled, attempting to call out through the swab that was suffocating her as he laid his weight down onto the girl, pinning her struggling body against the mattress.

Angry at being almost thwarted in his sick purpose, he clamped harder with the swab, pushing part of it into the girl's mouth, and within seconds felt her go limp beneath him. Caroline Dickinson would have passed out from a total lack of oxygen to the brain within just ten seconds, after which cerebral hypoxia would have caused the brain to cease all functions after approximately four minutes. After savagely raping his dying victim, the killer lifted himself up and zipped his trousers before leaving the room and closing the door behind him. Caroline Dickinson now lay dead between her sleeping companions. The time, confirmed by a teacher who saw the silhouette of a man pass her open door, was 5.00 am.

The schoolgirl from Cornwall was not Montes's first victim. The serial sexual predator had toured Europe for years taking advantage of the lax security at youth hostels to abuse and rape young occupants, earning himself a prison sentence in Germany in the 1980s for armed rape. Other convictions across Europe included two other counts of rape, two for indecent assault and one for theft.

Montes's eventual downfall came in March 2001 when a US Immigration Officer from Detroit read of the UK inquest into the death of Caroline Dickinson and noticed that the report mentioned Montes, a convicted serial rapist, as a suspect in the murder. The name bothered him until he recalled that a man bearing the name of Francisco Arce Montes had been arrested for a sexual assault at a youth hostel in Miami, Florida, earlier that year. Once made aware of the name, French police contacted the Miami Police Department who obtained DNA samples from their prisoner which proved to be a perfect match for those taken from the body of Caroline Dickinson.

Montes was extradited to France to stand trial and in June 2004 he was found guilty of Caroline's murder, which he has always insisted was an 'accident', and sentenced to 30 years' imprisonment. Various appeals against the sentence have proved unsuccessful. Inquiries into Montes's implication in other rapes and murders going back 20 years are continuing.

CHAPTER 17

THE GREEN RIVER
SERIAL KILLINGS

Washington State, USA, 1982–1998

'These dead women were just garbage to me'
                                    – Gary Leon Ridgeway.

The Green River is a tributary of the Columbia River flowing through Washington State in the north-west corner of the USA, close up to the Canadian border. The waterway is long, flowing south to meet the mighty Colorado River before the two conjoin to span the continent from north to south as far as Nevada. But in the early 1980s the northern stretches of the Green River were to provide the background for a horrific series of murders against young prostitutes by a crazed serial killer who would not be brought to justice until he had killed more than 48 times.

In the months of July and August of the long hot summer of 1982 five women were strangled to death and left in or near the Green River in King County, Washington. All five had a history of prostitution and at least four had disappeared from Pacific Highway South, an area notorious for prostitution activity. These murders were the community's first awareness that a serial killer was preying on young women. Four of these five women had been found in territory covered by the King County Sheriff's Office, the agency that would be responsible for investigating and solving the crimes.

The bodies of the first victims were discovered in terrifying circumstances by 41-year-old hobby fisherman Bob Ainsworth. This man was fishing just above where the river met the outer limits of the city of Seattle. It was a stretch of water that Ainsworth knew well but nothing could have prepared him for the horror that awaited him downstream. As his rubber raft rounded a rocky bend in the river, Ainsworth looked down into the clear water and prepared to fend his craft off from rocks that were lying just under the surface. Instead of rocks, his gaze was met by a pair of staring eyes belonging to a young black woman whose body was swaying beneath her in a macabre dance with the rippling current.

At first he recoiled in horror then decided that the apparition must be a mannequin thrown off the rocks above the river by children. He reached for his fishing gaffe and attempted to hook the figure towards him but it appeared to catch on a rock under the surface. The body rolled in the water and the face broke the surface, the eyes staring at him through a tangle of hair.

Overcome with sheer terror as it became apparent he was staring into the face of a corpse, Ainsworth slipped and fell as his body weight overturned the raft. Cold water closed over his head and the corpse moved towards him in a floating embrace. He screamed, his breath erupting in bubbles as he fought to free himself from the body, its lips pulled back in the rictus of death. Turning in the water, his heart threatened to fail him as he came face to face with another corpse that his frantic struggles seemed to have called forth from the river's depths. He splashed towards the shore and pulled himself, pale and trembling, onto the bank.

Help finally came in the form of a man cycling with his children along the riverbank who listened in amazement to Ainsworth's gibbered tale of horror before cycling off to alert the police of the wringing wet, apparent madman sitting at the river's edge. Within 20 minutes a disbelieving young police officer arrived at the scene and questioned the fisherman, who was slipping into shock. Shaking his head in incredulity the policeman waded into the shallows and groped beneath the surface. His face paled in horror as he pulled a dead woman to the surface and he immediately called for backup.

More horror was to greet the reinforcements when they arrived. A cordon was set up and a search of the area began. Within half an hour a detective discovered the body of a young nude black female lying in a grassy area no more than 30 feet from the water. She had been strangled to death, a pair of blue panties still knotted around her neck. Bruises on her arms and legs told of a desperate struggle for life. Unlike the river corpses whose swollen flesh told of several days of immersion, an examination on the scene by Chief Medical Examiner Donald Reay established that the woman, who would be identified as 16-year-old Opal Mills, had died within the preceding 24 hours.

Reay noted advanced decomposition on one of the

other river corpses, afterwards identified as Marcia Chapman, 31, and determined that she had been in the water for at least seven days. The third body was of another known prostitute, Cynthia Hinds, who had been missing for 48 hours. Autopsies of the dead women would later reveal a bizarre fact. Both Chapman and Hinds both had pyramid-shaped rocks lodged in their vaginas.

A month earlier a young girl named Wendy Lee Coffield had been found floating in the Green River. She had been strangled. Six months before the discovery of Coffield, children had also found the body of her friend, Leanne Wilcox, who had been reported missing with Coffield. She had been strangled on an empty lot a few miles from the river. Even closer in the police timescale, the nude corpse of Deborah Bonner had been discovered slumped over a drifting log in the river. She too had been strangled and all women showed signs of sexual intercourse before death. The reign of the Green River Killer had begun.

With the nightmare knowledge that a serial sexual predator was on the loose, Major Richard Kraske of the Criminal Investigation Division formed a task force of detectives led by Detective Dave Reichert. Also on board was FBI profiler John Douglas and investigator Bob Kepple, whose dogged detective work would send serial killer Ted Bundy to the electric chair in 1989. But even with experts of such calibre on board, the investigation floundered in processing the flood of evidence and witness statements that threatened to swamp the fledgling task force. The early 1980s were not a good era for forensic investigation. DNA science was still years into the future and prostitutes are notoriously reluctant to talk to policemen.

Over the next few years, despite exhaustive enquiries by the dedicated team of detectives, now known as the Green River Task Force, the bodies of more and more murder victims were found. Most of the bodies were nude and identification sometimes took months and even years. It was obvious that the killer was choosing his victims from among the transient prostitute community. Few were reported missing by colleagues and it was only when a mother or a friend left in charge of a motherless baby reported a missing person that police were able to match up a corpse with a name. Eventually the Task Force logged 49 victims in the two-year period between 1982 to 1984, yet only seven were listed as missing.

The size of the Task Force grew as more murders were discovered and the list of suspects escalated into the hundreds, yet nothing definitive was found to identify the killer of even one of the victims. In 1988, six years after Bob Ainsworth's horrific discoveries in the Green River, desperation and public pressure to find the killer prompted detectives to send samples taken from several victims to a private laboratory for DNA typing. However, based on the fledgling technology available at the time, no DNA profiles were obtained. Meanwhile the prostitute community took protective measures themselves, working within close proximity of each other and noting car registrations. Nevertheless, the killings continued and the tally of the dead mounted.

By 1992 budget demands had resulted in a drastic reduction of Task Force personnel. That year saw one detective remaining to handle cases and follow up the thousands of leads that flooded into the King County Sheriff's office. The detective left in charge was Tom

Jensen, a dogged veteran investigator who would leave no stone unturned in investigating a case, no matter how old. In 1991, hoping to take advantage of recent developments in DNA profiling, Jensen sent biological evidence from several of the victims to the Washington State Patrol Crime Laboratory, and scored a tentative match. The profile corresponded with that of a suspect who had previously been questioned by police. The man's name was Gary Leon Ridgeway.

Ridgeway had first come to the notice of the Task Force eight years earlier as a result of the disappearance of Marie Malvar. A witness reported that Ridgeway's truck was similar to the one in which he had seen Malvar on the night she disappeared, but his description of the driver as white with a moustache fitted hundreds of men in the Green River area. Ridgeway denied picking up the girl and the inquiry was dropped. However, his constant sightings around Pacific Highway South led to further questioning over the years and he was interviewed on multiple occasions. He admitted using prostitutes and even that he had once assaulted a prostitute who had bitten him during oral sex. He even passed a polygraph test when requested to do so.

In 1987 a search warrant was served as a matter of course on Ridgeway's home, work locker, and several vehicles to which he had access. Items seized were submitted to the Washington State Patrol Crime Laboratory where they were compared to samples taken from the Green River victims. One item would prove to be significant: a saliva sample taken from a paint mask that Ridgeway used in his work. That sample would lie on record until the laboratory tested biological evidence submitted by the diligent Detective Tom Jensen, fourteen years later.

DNA technology had advanced to the point that while routinely checking Jensen's evidence against old DNA results, lab technician Beverley Himick found that a partial male DNA profile on a vaginal swab taken from river victim Marcia Chapman back in 1982 matched Ridgeway's DNA profile. Further analysis of pubic hairs found on fellow victim Opal Mills confirmed Ridgeway's guilt. Spurred by the success of Himick's analysis, forensic scientist Jean Johnston also discovered a link between sperm samples taken from Green River victim Carol Christensen and Ridgeway's DNA profile. Ridgeway was arrested within 24 hours and the hunt for the Green River Killer was over. Ridgeway immediately protested his innocence of all charges and it was only as detectives started to delve into his past that the gruesome story became apparent.

Gary Ridgeway was born on 18 February 1949 and had moved with his parents to King County, Washington State, when he was 11. His parents bought a house close to Pacific Highway South, the area where the Green River Killer found most of his victims. Ridgeway was not a bright pupil and graduated from High School two years behind his grade. He worked briefly for a motor truck company and in 1969 entered military service in the US Navy. In 1970 he married his first wife. The marriage failed and Ridgeway would later blame the divorce on his wife's adultery while he was overseas. He constantly referred to his first wife as 'a whore' who wrecked his life. This may well have influenced his choice of victim.

After leaving the Navy in 1971 he started work as a painter at the Kenworth Truck Company where he had worked briefly before military service. The Kenworth Truck Company is located on East Marginal Way South, a few miles north of the stretch of Pacific Highway South where he later picked up many of his victims. He was to work for Kenworth for more than 30 years until his arrest on 30 November 2001.

He had remarried in 1973 and had a son with a woman who was to become a vital prosecution witness at his eventual trial. The second Mrs Ridgeway spoke of rough outdoor sex in which her husband liked to tie her up and of how he liked to stalk her through the forest. Once, she told investigators, he used a police-type hold to choke her, the method he used to murder his victims. She also spoke of Ridgeway returning home late at night wet and dirty. The couple divorced in 1981 and the wife was given custody of the son, whom Ridgeway was allowed to take to his home on alternate weekends.

Soon after his second divorce Ridgeway bought a house at 21859 Place South in King County. The house was just a short walk from the prostitute-infested area of Pacific Highway South – Ridgeway appeared to be setting up shop in his own doorway. He would later confess to detectives that he killed dozens of women here until he sold the property, along with its dark memories, in 1985.

His rampage continued but he was wary of discovery, often going through a transaction with a prostitute if he thought her friends were suspicious. He likened this to softening up the women for an eventual kill by acting like a regular 'john'. He also took to scattering false clues such as cigarette butts and chewing gum around the sites where he dumped the bodies. In interviews he later told detectives that he only ever killed street prostitutes because they were easy victims. Prostitutes, he told police, were frequently on the move and 'no one gave a damn about them anyway'.

He compared his victims to garbage, telling police that he dumped them like he'd dispose of a sack of rubbish. But there was an even sicker side to Gary Ridgeway that would even make his hardened interrogators blanche. Ridgeway was a necrophile who often returned to have sex with his victim's corpse, on one occasion keeping a body in his truck and having sex with it during a lunch break at Kenworth. Some of the corpses, he admitted, were in an advanced stage of decomposition.

Most of Ridgeway's victims were in their teens and who, he insisted, were less likely to be suspicious of him and also, he hinted, were liable to plead more earnestly for their lives. Most of his victims were white but he seemed indifferent to race. A chilling transcript from his trial reads: 'I'd much rather have white, but black was fine. It's just... just garbage. Just somethin' to screw and kill her and dump her.' Just as coldly the transcript tells of his method of killing his victims: 'I'd tell her I could only get off if I did her from behind. That way she'd raise her head when she thought I'd finished and I could get my arm around her neck and squeeze until she stopped struggling.'

As stated earlier, Ridgeway used a police choke-hold to kill his victims, locking their neck into the crook of his elbow and using his other arm to apply pressure, causing unconsciousness in ten seconds. Death would follow swiftly as the brain shut down through lack of oxygen. Nevertheless, although Ridgeway admitted to killing over 60 women, due to lack of solid evidence the prosecution could proceed in only four cases. These were those of Cynthia Hinds, Marcia Chapman, Carol Christensen, and Opal Mills. In three of those four cases DNA evidence linked Ridgeway to the victims. The body of Cynthia Hinds was found near enough to two of the other victims to leave no doubt that the same killer had committed the crime. On 5 December 2001, counts of Aggravated Murder in the First Degree were entered against Ridgeway in all four cases.

Four out of 60 possible counts of murder did not satisfy the regrouped Task Force who now began to review and investigate the remaining cases for further forensic study with a view to lining up more charges against the man recognised to be the most prolific serial killer in the history of the nation. Meanwhile, the King County Superior Court set a charging deadline to ensure that the trial of Gary Ridgeway went ahead without undue prosecution delays. The date set was 28 March 2003.

Shortly before the deadline, clothing of two as yet unprocessed victims, Wendy Coffield and Debra Estes, sent to private laboratory Microtrace, revealed tiny spheres of sprayed paint residue identical to the highly specialised Du Pont Imron paint used at the Kenworth plant where Ridgeway worked.

Of the total of five murdered women left in or near Green River within a 28-day period between July and August of 1982, Wendy Coffield was the first and Ridgeway was already charged with killing the last three victims. It was obvious to the detectives that the killer of these four women had also killed victim Debra Bonner, whose nude body was found in the Green River a few weeks after Coffield's and only a few days before the discovery, prompted by fisherman Bob Ainsworth, of Mills, Hinds, and Chapman. Three additional counts of Aggravated Murder in the First Degree for Wendy Coffield, Debra Bonner, and Debra Estes were hurriedly entered against Ridgeway in the eleventh hour of 27 March, 24 hours before the charging deadline expired.

The killer's cockiness had faded in April 2002 when the King County Prosecuting Attorney, Norm Maleg, issued written notice that he would be seeking the death penalty. Now almost a year later, Ridgeway was facing seven counts of Aggravated Murder, each of which could cause him death on the lethal injection table, despite the fact that he would be paying for no more than a fraction of the Green River slayings. Subsequent to the second arraignment, Ridgeway's defence team approached the prosecution to ask whether Maleg would forego seeking the death penalty in exchange for Ridgeway's pleas of guilty on all seven charged counts, plus 40 to 47 additional counts of murder. Ridgeway also undertook to provide a complete account of each murder and to direct investigators to the graves of a number of his victims.

Maleg made his decision. By accepting the proposal of Ridgeway's defence team, the truth about the Green River killings would be made public and the community's enduring nightmare would be over. In addition, Ridgeway would be held accountable for every murder he had committed and families of the victims would find a measure of justice and resolution. By agreeing to the plea bargain, Ridgeway could not appeal his sentence and would die in prison. Justice would be served.

In all, Gary Ridgeway claimed to have killed over 60 women in King County. In addition he identified several sites where victims had been dumped from murders not attributed to the Green River Killer. Some of the remains recovered at some sites identified by Ridgeway have not been identified to this day. Interviews with Ridgeway lasted for four months in which detectives and profilers were able to study the mind of a prolific serial killer. At first insisting he had stopped killing in 1985 when he met his present wife, as the interviews progressed the last year he killed changed from 1985 to 1987 and onwards through 1991 to 1998 up to some indefinite time before his arrest in 2001. He also admitted pride in his murders, insisting he would not claim to have killed a woman unless he had done so. He explained his reasons with a bizarre stab at professional integrity: 'Why, if it isn't mine? Because I have a pride in... in... what I do. I don't wanna take it from anybody else.'

One reason put forward by crime specialists in answer to why Ridgeway escaped detection for so long is that he did not fit the popular preconceptions of a serial killer. The case of the Green River Killer became a cautionary tale around the offices of profilers at the FBI's establishment at Quantico. The preconceptions Ridgeway did not fit included the fact that he was not a loner, he controlled his anger, and had no known significant juvenile or violent criminal history. He had also been married or with a steady girlfriend throughout most, if not all, of his adult life. He was steadily employed for 30 years and had received an award at Kenworth's for his

·perfect attendance record. Even after his arrest in 2001, long-time work colleagues, former girlfriends, and family members expressed doubt that he could be a killer. In short, those who thought they knew Ridgeway best didn't know him at all.

Gary Leon Ridgeway was sentenced on 18 December 2003 to 48 life sentences with no possibility of parole. In addition, Judge Richard Jones imposed an extra 10 years on each count for tampering with evidence, adding another 480 years. He also sentenced Ridgeway to an additional life sentence to be served consecutively. A more recent count of victims of the Green River Killer brings the current figure to 71.

The world's most prolific serial killer is reputed to be Pedro Alonso López, who is serving a life sentence after confessing to the murders of 300 pre-teen girls in Peru, Colombia, and Ecuador in the 1970s.

CHAPTER 18

MURDER AT JONESTOWN

Guyana, Northern South America, 18 November 1978

'We must make the supreme sacrifice'
   – The Reverend James Warren Jones.

The stench was an impenetrable miasma stirred by the whirling blades of the helicopter. Below, bloated bodies stretched like a bizarre carpet, its pattern irregular and broken into clusters of colour by the bright clothes of the victims. Nine hundred and twelve bodies were strewn in haphazard order on the ground around the broad roof of the communal meeting place. The bodies had lain untouched and unmoved for two days – until news of the Jonestown massacre had been spread by the fleeing members of Senator Leon Ryan's fact-finding mission to the settlement of the Peoples Temple in Guyana, the former Dutch and English colony on the northern coast of South America.

They had escaped death by gunfire but the pathetic clumps of corpses below – mothers clutching children, fathers proffering redundant protective arms – had died from mass poisoning by order of the man they referred to as 'Pop'. That man was James Warren (Jim) Jones, their spiritual leader, founder and pastor of their religious movement that recognised no god but him and accepted no other dogma. Jim Jones himself had been shot in the head by a 9 mm bullet and his body lay sprawled in an armchair in a central position under the roof of the communal meeting place.

We all have occasional delusions of grandeur. It might be while driving the hire car that is two steps up from our original clunker or being noticed by a celebrity to whom we once delivered a package. Jim Jones of Indiana deluded himself and the nearly 1000 people who believed he represented God on Earth, while also being involved in a theft of US government funds of staggering proportions. It was to end in death for over 900 of his followers and for Jones himself, betrayed in the eleventh hour by one of his own henchmen. Up to the time of the terrorist attack that brought down New York's Trade Centre, it represented the biggest loss of American citizen civilian life in US history.

The death toll at the camp in Guyana in 1978 was reported at the time as a mass suicide by devoted followers of the 'Reverend Jim', in despair at an interfering world that would not let them survive. Recent research has shown it to be anything but. The massacre at Jonestown was mass murder.

James Warren Jones was born in Crete, Indiana, on 13 May 1931. When his parents separated during the Great Depression of the 1930s he moved with his mother to

Richmond, Indiana, where he graduated with honours from Richmond High in 1948. As a child, the young James was obsessed with his perception of religion, often killing small animals so that he could perform funeral rites over their graves. Despite having become a member of the US Communist party in 1951, Jones flirted with the Methodist Church and seemed intrigued by religious worship. He exhibited unpopular liberal leanings at a time when the southern USA was struggling under the Kennedy administration to shake off the shadow of racial segregation.

Jones became a student pastor for the Methodists but later resigned after an argument with the church elders over his recruitment of blacks and other ethnic groups to his congregation – Jones often boasted of his own Cherokee origins through his mother, but he owed this more to his natural swarthy appearance than any ethnic roots bestowed by the austere Lynetta Putnam Jones. Forsaking his American Communist Party membership when the ACP expressed its distaste at Soviet excesses under Stalin, Jones became interested in the financial possibilities offered by religion after witnessing a session of faith healing at a local gospel church.

In 1955 he founded his own church, The Wings of Deliverance, soon to be renamed as The Peoples' Temple Christian Church Full Gospel, presumably in case anyone missed the point. He became active in human rights, even being appointed in 1960 as director of Human Rights by Indianapolis Democratic Mayor Charles Boswell, who was to figure prominently in Jones's future plans. Jones's activity in human rights issues annoyed many of his contemporaries at a time when the US southern states were meeting their own nemesis on black integration into society. In retrospect, some of Jones's liberal activities seem self-serving but there is no doubt that he was at the forefront of the black struggle against repression, even acting as an unpaid orderly and changing bedpans in a blacks' ward of the local hospital, where he had been mistakenly admitted due to his dark skin tone after a mild heart attack.

Jones had married in 1949 and he and his wife Marceline, who was an ex-nurse, also adopted children of mixed race. Jones referred to them as his 'Rainbow Family'. In 1961, soon after the foundation of the renamed Peoples Temple, Jones and his wife became the first white couple to adopt a black child, a move which earned them physical abuse and recrimination from among the redneck community that still flew the Confederate flag on their porches and had pictures of Robert E Lee pinned to their walls.

Jones and his family then moved to the more amenable California. But Jones had a secret. What his opponents in Indianapolis had seen as a 'nigger-loving preacher' was in fact an ardent communist who saw religion only as a way to advance his own anti-capitalist dogmas. Jones also saw other advantages, recalling the donations he had seen flowing in at the faith healing session he had witnessed. As membership of his Church grew, Jones realised there was no future for fully developing his plans of a malleable society in the USA and he began to seek a haven abroad where he could settle his New World colony.

For years, in keeping with his master plan developed as he watched the faith healer at work so many years ago, Jones had been playing the political card in California with his followers as the collateral. Membership of the Peoples Temple had reached 20,000 by the early 1970s and, acting on the word of their beloved 'Pop', his congregation put their votes where he directed. Thirteen buses were on constant stand-by to transport large groups of people to political rallies favoured by Jones. In the 1975 San Francisco mayoral campaign of George Moscone, Temple members were on hand to vote in precinct after precinct to ensure Moscone's victory. Ordered by Jones, Temple voters went from area to area voting many times over, where Temple members employed as polling officials failed to confiscate voting cards that were repeatedly reused. Despite the fact that more votes were registered than the electoral roll, Moscone was elected and prepared to return the favour to Jones and his Temple.

Jones's un-Christian sentiments became clear when Moscone's thwarted opponent, John Barbagelata, lodged a complaint of voter fraud. Jones sent him a consolation box of chocolates that also contained a bomb. The bomb was primed to do little damage but nonetheless Mr Barbagelata swiftly withdrew his objections and welcomed Moscone in office. Moscone's ascent to power was swiftly followed by the appointment of Timothy Stoen, a Jones lieutenant, as San Francisco Assistant District Attorney with charge of the Voters Fraud Investigation Unit. Ballot forms promptly disappeared and no one was charged. Jones himself became Head of San Francisco Housing Authority.

Aided by Temple members in local government in both Peoples Temple locations of Ukiah and San Francisco, placed by his political nominees, Jones was able to manipulate state benefit payouts to his church members, cash that was passed to the Temple. One method was by arranging adoption of orphans to Temple members for which state benefits were paid; additional profit was gained by sending the children out to beg for the Temple. Jones's housing appointment allowed him to place Temple members in free accommodation simply by removing certain housing projects and repossessed property from the general housing allocation lists. These properties were then registered as Peoples Temple properties, tax-exempt for rent or sale under the Temple's religious IRS classification.

But with criticism from the press, which reported stories from worried family members of Jones's devotees, plus pressure from Republicans aware of Jones's electoral chicanery and a threatened investigation by the IRS, Jones searched for an idyllic enclave far from the reach of the Temple's burgeoning critics, an enclave that would exist on the flood of state benefits provided by the politicians he had helped place in power with the promise of his proxy electorate ready to come to their aid in US elections. His utopian dream was of a pseudo-religious empire modelled on a merger of religion and politics.

At first he and Marceline looked at Brazil but bureaucratic problems plus difficulties with the Portuguese language forced them to look further afield. The Cooperative Republic of Guyana had a socialist ring to the name that attracted the couple, and Jim Jones entered into negotiation with the government of the former British colony where English was spoken as the everyday language. Jones was correct in his assumption of socialism. Guyana's prime minister, Forbes Burnham, was a committed socialist who believed co-operatives were the political way forward.

The Peoples Temple negotiated a lease with Burnham's government for 4000 acres of jungle land and construction began with prefabricated housing erected by imported Temple workmen under the title of the Peoples Temple Agricultural Project. As well as construction material imported from the United States, Jones brought in firearms to police his kingdom and a staple to dominate the community and feed his own growing heroin and cocaine drug dependency. Jonestown was eventually policed by hand-picked thugs armed with rifles, shotguns, and pistols. A special detachment of the most vicious formed Jones's personal bodyguard. Another deal with Forbes Burnham struck in exchange for the promise of massive investment of Temple funds in the country, saw Guyanan immigration policy aimed at denying entry visas to Jones's investigators and critics.

At first, Jonestown flourished on the surface. Mass immigration unimpeded by Guyana authorities saw the colony thrive. The poor, infertile soil was made to yield fruit and vegetables by the settlers' labour and that which wasn't produced locally was imported for sale in community shops. But the idyll faded as drugs were sold and distributed openly along with alcohol – Jones was aware of the lessons learned in Stalin's Russia: keep the peasants poor, docile, and dependent upon authority. Jones and his henchmen forcibly took young women from among the community as their concubines and no one dared protest.

Justice was brutal, with Jones as the supreme judge of the community court, ruling life or death as it suited his purpose. No one was allowed to leave and an escapee's exit from Guyana was barred by the country's immigration police. By 1978 Forbes Burnham was blissfully aware that in Jones's congregation he had nearly 1000 votes pledged to his Peoples National Congress Party.

Under Jones's rule, Temple members worked six days a week from 6.30 am to 6.00 pm with an hour for lunch. Evenings were spent attending rallies at which Jim Jones spoke of the wonders of communism and the power of revolution. Many of those who had joined the temple with a view to embracing Christ found they were embracing Jim Jones and the Soviet Union instead. Discontent was common, spoken in undertones, for no one dared oppose Jones's corrupted and drug-ridden regime. Jonestown's radio towers rang daily with the speeches of Jim Jones and his wife Marceline railing against capitalism and the United States. The welfare cheques rolled in, handed in to be cashed and retained by the Temple on arrival. About this time, large amounts of cash were transported in suitcases to accounts in Zurich and Paris by Jones's mistress, Terri Buford, the Temple's financial manager. These accounts totalled US$26 million and were all in Buford's name. The cash was embezzled from the local governments of Ukiah and San Francisco as well as social security payments accrued from Temple members. The Jones's financial machine also claimed for those who had died in the USA. Hospital records and obituary columns were scanned for the names of the recently deceased and credit cards and benefits applied for in their names. But the clouds were darkening over Jones's empire. Relatives of the temple cult, alarmed at reports of brainwashing and concentration-camp conditions at Jonestown, now turned to the US government for action, and California Congressman Leo Ryan embarked on the fact-finding mission to Guyana that would lead to his death and the dissolution of the Temple.

Ryan and his party arrived at the Port Kaituma airstrip, a few miles outside Jonestown, on 18 November 1978. The party included Ryan aide Jackie Speier, US Embassy representative Dick Dwyer, nine journalists, and four concerned relatives of Temple members. The congressman's declared mission was to survey Jonestown and interview some of its inhabitants. The day did not go well and tempers became heated when some of Jonestown's discontented inhabitants took courage at the congressman's presence and told him they wished to leave. Their departure was opposed by Jones and his guards and the situation deteriorated until Ryan, responding to a death threat by a Temple guard, decided to cut short his visit and return to the USA, taking with him 14 Temple members who wished to leave. Ryan's plane was not big enough to take everyone and another aircraft was ordered from Kaituma. Among the party of Temple defectors was Larry Leyton, whose request for defection had aroused the suspicion of the other discontented defectors since he was a known henchman of Jones. No one is sure whether Jones himself gave the order or whether some of his guards took it upon themselves to prevent Ryan's departure. A hazy video reproduction of the attack at the airstrip by Jones's armed guards records only shots fired at the party until the camera falls to the ground as the cameraman is shot. Leo Ryan died, shot in the face and body multiple times by Leyton who, on boarding the plane, had turned a handgun on his fellow passengers. This acted as a signal for other guards who had accompanied the party to the airport to fire on both aircraft, killing three journalists, and a defector. Surviving members of the congressman's party fled into the surrounding jungle.

News of the botched killings sent Jones into a paroxysm of rage. He screamed at his henchmen that the death of Ryan would make it impossible for the commune to continue functioning. The Peoples Temple would become a pariah in Guyana and a return to the United States was now out of the question. The word of 'Pop' was that members of the Peoples Temple must make the ultimate sacrifice and demonstrate their brutal treatment at the hands of the US government by dying together in a 'roar' of silent protest at the cruelty of their situation.

The community were to die by drinking a mixture of Kool-Aid – a commercial fruit flavoured soft drink – cyanide, sedatives, and tranquillisers. Jones pledged to join them but one might suspect from evidence found at the scene that he planned to flee during the orgy of death and join Terri Buford, who was a notable survivor of the massacre. There were other survivors. Armed guards stood ready to shoot anyone who attempted to escape before, presumably, drinking the mixture themselves, but some disillusioned cult members managed to hide or escape into the jungle, emerging only when the poison had wreaked its devastation.   One old dear, enjoying her afternoon nap, slept through the entire event and woke up to find her sister and some friends dead on the floor. Marcy Jones was found dead near the community centre, a letter at her side asking that all bank assets in her name should go to the Communist Party of the USSR. Jim Jones was found dead in his armchair, shot through the head. The gun that killed him was found 60 feet from his body, possibly abandoned by the killer who had effected his own version of justice and thwarted Jones's plans for escape and life with Terri Buford and $26 million. Alternatively, the weapon might have been dropped by whoever Jones had asked to kill him – or by somebody who knew the location of that fortune in US dollars.

News of the Ryan killing reached the outside world later that day and a detachment of the Guyana Army was despatched to investigate. It reached Jonestown early the next morning and was met by flocks of vultures and cawing crows circling over the scenes of death. A search team found US$3 million in cash hidden in Jones's prefabricated bungalow. In an interview given later by Terri Buford, it was claimed to be cash set aside to pay for mafia death contracts on Jones's enemies after his death. Two defectors who escaped during the airport shootings confirmed that Jones 'often boasted of his mafia contacts'. Nine days after Jones's death Mayor Moscone was murdered, along with Harvey Milk, a politician who had originally been a staunch Temple insider but had disassociated himself at the onset of enquiries into Jones's affairs.

Milk had often told police that Jonestown politicians were planning to kill him to ensure his silence. He had been correct in his assumption and was shot to death on 27 November, the same day that Mayor Moscone met his fate. A man named Dan White was arrested for their murders. White confessed that he had shot Moscone because he feared the mayor would not re-hire him for his supervisory post in the wake of Jones's death. White had in fact resigned the post voluntarily on the day congressman Leo

Ryan announced his fact-finding trip to Jonestown. White left prison in 1988 having served five years, and was found dead in his car less than two months later. His death was never fully investigated.

Buford also alleged that the apparent mass suicide at Jonestown had been orchestrated by Jones and his political conspirators to steal the hidden millions concealed in European bank accounts. The ex-Temple financial manager labelled the suicides as mass murder, pointing out that many Temple members who had not drunk the Kool-Aid concoction had been shot, some by crossbows, a weapon not generally favoured by suicides. Buford alleged that Jones had planned to escape with his guards in a helicopter waiting in the jungle but was killed by former bodyguard Michael Stokes as he sat in a drug-induced stupor while his former congregation died around him. Stokes had been Buford's lover until Jones took her from him, perhaps leaving Stokes thirsting for revenge at the first opportunity.

What happened after is open to speculation and relies on Buford's statements to investigators. Buford claims to have escaped the killing of 18 November and to have contacted Jones's lawyer, Mark Lane. Lane had himself escaped from Jonestown some days earlier with a colleague after Jones accused him of not working in the Temple's best interests. Lane had achieved a certain notoriety in the USA with his conspiracy theories on the deaths of J F Kennedy and Martin Luther King, twenty years earlier. According to Buford, Lane's role in the Jonestown administration had been to shift the blame for excesses by Jones and his associates to the CIA.

Lane represented Buford during her investigation by US

authorities and the couple eventually became lovers. They had a daughter, and pillow talk during their relationship resulted in Lane receiving full details of the hidden bank accounts. In a TV interview a few months after Lane broke off the relationship, he denied any personal involvement with Buford. The money has never been traced. Terri Buford subsequently went into hiding soon after, citing fear for her life from Jones's political allies, whose careers would be in jeopardy if their connections with Jim Jones should be made public.

In his book on the Jonestown conspiracy, Pulitzer Prizewinner Tim Reiterman revealed that the US House Foreign Affairs Committee questioned Terri Buford behind closed doors and later sealed the documents. The depths of corruption that permeated California politics in the 1970s remain uncovered to this day, buried with the bones of 912 members of Jim Jones's Peoples Temple who believed in 'Pop'... until it cost them their lives.

CHAPTER 19

THE WASHINGTON SNIPER

Washington DC, USA, 2–22 October 2002

'The time had come for jihad against the West'
— John Allen Muhammad.

The Blue Chevrolet Caprice in the Shoppers Food Warehouse parking lot in Glenmont was at least 12 years old and looked like anybody's average clunker. The coachwork was dusty, the tyres under-inflated, and the teenage black kid sitting at the wheel looked like a thousand others, full-lipped and apparently slack-jawed as he lay back in the seat and watched the world from under heavy-lidded eyes.

An alert observer walking near the Chevrolet might have noticed something slightly out of kilter with the registration plate. It appeared to be hanging loose from the boot surface and jutting out at an angle as if hinged at the bottom. Looking closer, behind the plate was a hole of 10 cms square, now exposed. Another hole was cut above it. The Chevrolet suddenly started up and moved forwards a few feet before reversing back on a slightly different wheel lock as if seeking a better angle of parking. A blue steel barrel emerged a few inches from the hole in the boot and the sharp flat bark of a .223 calibre rifle was flung back as an echo from the perimeter wall surrounding the asphalt parking space off the Washington DC Beltway.

Again the engine of the Chevrolet was started up, the exhaust a white mist against the chill October air of autumn in the USA's northerly latitudes. The teenager drove the car slowly out of the car park and turned right. One hundred metres away in the south of the car park shoppers stared in horror at the body of an elderly man lying against the driver's door of his vehicle, his shopping spread around him on the asphalt, already staining with the deep scarlet of his lifeblood. The victim was 55-year-old Jim Martin, a systems analyst. The time was 6.30 pm. The Washington Sniper had claimed his first victim in Montgomery County Maryland. Some onlookers would remember a bright red splash on the victim's coat seconds before they heard the shot and saw him fall.

The shooter at the food-hall car park was John Allen Muhammad, a 41-year-old Muslim convert who had changed his surname from Williams on his conversion. Earlier that day Muhammad had fired a single shot that shattered the window of a nearby craft store, no doubt testing the disguise and method to be used in later shootings. Together with his Jamaican teenage accomplice, Lee Boyd Malvo, Muhammad had converted the boot and back seat of the Chevrolet Caprice to allow him to lie prone in a sniping position with the barrel of the rifle, a Bushmaster .223 calibre XM15, similar to the US military

M16, supported on a bipod and extending through a hole hidden behind the hinged registration plate. Above, another hole allowed a view through the telescopic sight. The aiming point of the rifle was a laser marker that would splash a red dot on the target. Depending on calculations made for the distance of the shot, wherever the dot fell, the bullet would strike.

Muhammad was a negro born in Baton Rouge, Louisiana, who had served in the US military during the Second Gulf War as a National Guardsman, receiving his discharge as a sergeant in 1994. He had joined the Louisiana National Guard in 1978, eventually volunteering for active duty that took him to Iraq. Though not a sniper, he had obtained a top marksman grade with a rifle on the range. Oddly, he had joined the Nation of Islam movement before his service in the Gulf and one can only speculate at his motives in volunteering for active service abroad. Certainly, following his arrest, drawings found by police among the belongings of Lee Malvo, his teenage accomplice, appeared to point to the shootings as *jihad* against the West. A darker motive was put forward by Muhammad's ex-wife who believed the shootings to be part of a plot to kill her and gain custody of their children by including her as a casual victim. Malvo, while quite happy to go along with the idea of *jihad* also believed that a demand would be made by Muhammad on the US government for US$10 million to stop the shootings, the money going to fund training camps for young blacks 'somewhere in Canada'.

For whatever reason, the reign of the Washington Sniper had begun two weeks before the Food Warehouse incident, when a botched robbery in Montgomery, Alabama, left one woman dead and another injured after a hold-up of a liquor store. Muhammad would later boast of this shooting and taunt police in phone calls, acts that would later put them on his trail. Muhammad's accomplice in the liquor store hold-up was 17-year-old Malvo, whom he had met in Antigua while living there following his discharge from the National Guard.

Muhammad formed a relationship with Malvo's mother, Una, who left the teenager with Muhammad when she entered the USA illegally in 2000. A year later Muhammad and Malvo followed her, and mother and son were both eventually apprehended by Border Police in Washington.

After his release on a bond, Malvo absconded and joined Muhammad, ingeniously changing his name from Lee Boyd Malvo to Tommy Lee Malvo in an attempt to put Immigration off the track. Since Immigration didn't bother to look for him, the ruse was successful. Malvo and Muhammad's relationship from that point on is open to question. There is no doubt that Malvo worshipped his pseudo guardian but speculation that a homosexual relationship was formed between them has been raised by investigators. It was while the pair were living together in Tacoma, Washington DC, that Malvo stole the Bushmaster XM-15 rifle from a gun store, possibly on Muhammad's orders. The plan to terrorise the nation's capital was underway.

As a child, Muhammad had watched the final moments of New Orleans sniper Black Panther, Mark Essex, on television. Essex had been trapped on the roof of the city's Howard Johnson Hotel and the NBC audience watched the drama unfold as Essex died in hail of bullets in a final exchange with police. After Muhammad's arrest, a battery of psychiatrists would put forward the Mark Essex episode as a possible reason for the sniper shootings in Washington. There is no doubt that both shooters chose their victims by race. Both men's victims were white and fell in the category of the Middle American WASP – White Anglo Saxon Protestant. Both men had a committed hatred of the white community.

During his lethal spree, Essex killed nine people, injuring 13. Muhammad's goal was much higher. Malvo told police that his mentor planned to kill six people a day. Muhammad's final count was 16 dead and four injured. Only a few escaped the marksmanship of the man who had left the National Guard with the badge of Expert Rifleman. Five people died by his hand on 3 October, the day following the killing of Jim Martin.

Sarah Ramos, Jim Buchanan, Premkumar Walekar, Lori Ann Lewis-Rivera, and Pascal Chariot all died of a single bullet wound, each one dying of one of the five shots fired from the Bushmaster XM-15 in Maryland on that day. The following day, Caroline Seawell of Fredericksburg, Virginia, survived a shooting and Muhammad's aim deserted him three days later in Bowie, Maryland when 13-year-old Iran Brown was wounded by the gunman but survived. Muhammad moved on to Virginia, killing three and wounding one, before returning to Maryland to claim the life of Conrad Johnson, his last victim.

Throughout the sniper's three-week reign of terror – when anyone could expect the slamming force of a gunshot blow to the body or head – residents around the Washington Beltway, the interstate highway 495 that circles Washington DC and its inner suburbs in Maryland

and Virginia, moved around in fear. No one walked in lighted areas at night and people were fearful of using shopping mall car parks or of filling their cars at gas stations. The shots came out of the blue with no warning and the sniper's aim was deadly. What had begun with a bullet through the window of a Maryland craft store escalated into the largest manhunt that the area had ever seen. Police called on the public to be vigilant and circulated a description of a white van with black lettering seen in the area around the shootings. One person reported a 'grey' car fleeing the scene but without a registration number the description was of no use. 'All cars are grey in the dark,' remarked one investigator.

But the Washington sniper would be trapped by the 'death wish' of all serial killers – to taunt their pursuers. It came from Muhammad in the form of a telephone call boasting of a previous killing. The caller told police to take a look at an unsolved murder case in Montgomery, the site of the botched hold-up of a liquor store in which a woman had died. Police immediately went over records for the town named, concentrating on Montgomery County, Maryland and overlooking Montgomery, Alabama, where the fatal shooting had in fact taken place. It wasn't until a priest told police of a strange confessional telephone call in which a man with a southern state accent had mentioned the killing of a woman in Montgomery, Alabama, that investigators realised their mistake and contacted police in Alabama.

Alabama police recalled the incident in which the two suspects had narrowly avoided capture when fleeing after the shooting. No one had been caught but the Washington investigators were in luck – a partial fingerprint had been lifted from the scene and identified as belonging to Lee Malvo, courtesy of the Immigration and Naturalisation database, recorded after the detention of Malvo and his mother in 2002. Delving into Malvo's background, investigators discovered a link between Malvo and Muhammad, previously named Williams.

Muhammad, officers learned, was a Gulf war veteran known for his affiliations to militant Islamic groups, and an expert marksman to boot. Things were looking up for the investigation. More luck followed: traffic police had come across Muhammad sleeping in a car in a routine traffic check in north-west Baltimore on 8 October, the day after the near-fatal wounding of schoolboy Iran Brown. The vehicle in which Muhammad slept was a 1990 Chevrolet Caprice with New Jersey registration plates. Muhammad was alone in the vehicle at the time of the traffic stop but the traffic officer's suspicions were aroused because the man's driving licence showed a Washington State address, while the car was registered in New Jersey. However, a quick check showed the driver had no outstanding warrants so he was allowed to leave. The link between Muhammad and the Chevrolet were to prove crucial to the investigators, who up to that point had been searching for white vans that didn't exist.

The net was closing. Police now had Muhammad in a recognisable vehicle in the general vicinity of the shootings and now turned to phone records to link previous sightings of the car with payphone locations used by the sniper. The hammer fell when a 1990 Chevrolet Caprice with the New Jersey licence plate of NDA 21Z was seen in the Ashland area soon after the shooting of Jeffrey Hopper at 8.00 pm on 19 October.

Mr Hopper was gunned down in a hurried shooting outside the Ponderosa steakhouse and was one of the four Sniper victims to survive. The licence plate registration and a description of the vehicle was released to the media and an arrest warrant was issued for Muhammad for 'unrelated firearm violations'.

On Thursday 24 October, truck driver Ron Lantz pulled into a rest stop in Maryland, 50 miles from Washington, and nearly collided with a poorly parked blue Chevrolet. The occupants, two black men, were asleep in the front seats. Lantz noticed the registration plate and paled. Slowly and as quietly as the truck's rattling engine would allow, he reversed back onto the highway and put distance between his truck and the rest stop before finding a payphone kiosk.

Armed officers and a Washington Police SWAT team descended on the Caprice an hour later. Muhammad and Malvo awoke bleary eyed to find themselves the wrong end of a dozen automatic firearms and surrendered peacefully. Officers examined the car and found a Bushmaster rifle, a telescopic scope, and a bipod. A box of ammunition contained 20 rounds of .223 calibre Hornady V-Max bullets. The soft-nose bullet, christened 'Cop Killer' in underworld slang, is a particularly nasty round that expands on contact, ripping through flesh in its malformed state to cause horrific injuries. Unlike the full-metal-jacket round, it seldom exits the body and remains inside the victim.

A SWAT officer at the scene described the Chevrolet as a 'killing machine'. The two holes in the boot were for the rifle and the scope, and the back seat had been altered to fold down, allowing a potential shooter to lie fully extended when taking the shot. The rifle would later be linked to two other killings and all but three of the Sniper shootings, the rounds recovered in the latter cases being too distorted to make an effective match for ballistics.

After the arrests, Lee Malvo was initially charged with absconding after being released on bond by the Immigration and Naturalisation Department, but this charge was later dropped in favour of the murder of FBI analyst Linda Franklin at Falls Church Virginia on 14 October, and the murders of 'more than one person' in a three-year period. Another charge referred to the illegal use of a firearm in the murder of Franklin.

Malvo spent his initial months of custody in Fairfax County Prison, Virginia. His defence team chosen by the court would later plead that he was not guilty of all charges by reason of insanity, since he was under the complete domination and control of Muhammad. Malvo in the meantime told the prosecution that he 'wanted to kill everyone'. As is usual when the method of killings may have stirred local public emotions, the defence pleaded for a change of venue and Malvo's trial was moved to Chesapeake, 150 miles away. The defence rested its case on the teenager's indoctrination into militant Islam by Muhammad. In December 2003, over a year after his arrest, Malvo received a sentence of life without parole. Cases still remained on record and further charges against Malvo were pending.

The possibility of a death sentence for further charges of murder caused Malvo's defence to enter a plea bargain in respect of the murder of Kenneth Bridges and the attempted murder of Caroline Seawell. Such a plea, referred to in US legal terms as an 'Alford Plea' – using precedence established in the case of North Carolina versus Alford – meant that while not admitting guilt of the act, the defendant accepts that sufficient circumstantial evidence exists to prove guilt and therefore throws in the towel. It is a fact that the US Supreme Court now rules against the death penalty for crimes committed when aged under 18, but that decision was made in 2005, a year after Malvo's trial.

At 42, Muhammad was not to be so lucky. Anxious to spare himself the death penalty, his erstwhile companion told investigators the whole story. Malvo was finally charged with six more murders in Maryland and pleaded guilty to all, finally receiving six more consecutive life sentences without the possibility of parole. Meanwhile, Muhammad went on trial 200 miles away in Virginia Beach. Acting with the arrogance that was to dominate all his appearances in court, Muhammad dismissed his legal counsel and presented his own opening argument that was so erratic and poorly received that he opted to re-engage counsel immediately after.

He was charged with murder, conspiracy, terrorism, and the illegal use of firearms. More than 130 witnesses were called to place Muhammad at the scene of some of the murders. For a while, a legal argument raged that Malvo and not Muhammad had pulled the trigger under a bizarre Virginian law which held that only a gunman could be held guilty of criminal murder and not those who assisted in the crime. The law was later hurriedly repealed.

On 17 November 2003, John Allen Muhammad was found guilty on all counts entered against him in Virginia and he was sentenced to death. Other charges in other states followed and the guilty tally rose, by now redundant, since the perpetrator had been condemned to die, but the law likes to leave no loose ends. On 10 November 2009, Muhammad was put to death by lethal injection. An appeal for clemency, entered the previous day by his legal team, had been denied. The gun shop from which the Bushmaster rifle had been stolen by Malvo and Bushmaster Firearms Incorporated were parties to a US$2.5 million out-of-court settlement to two of Muhammad's injured victims and the families of victims who had filed complaints in the tort suit brought against them in a Legal Action Project to prevent gun violence by the Brady Centre.

Muhammad died with no word of remorse for his victims, and his actions, following so closely on the heels of the fundamentalist attack on New York in September 2001, were seen as part of the growing *jihad* against America and the West.

CHAPTER 20

9/11 THE WORLD TRADE CENTER

New York, USA, 11 September 2001

'Are you ready? Let's roll!'
 — The last words heard of Flight 193
 passenger Todd Beamer.

At 40 seconds past 8.46 Eastern Standard Time (EST) an American Airlines Boeing 767-223ER, registration N334NA, hurtled low over the skies of New York and impacted with the North Tower of the World Trade Center site in Lower Manhattan. The aircraft, scheduled as AA Flight 11, was travelling at around 450 mph and carried a fuel load of 10,000 US gallons. All 92 people aboard died as well as many in the building.

At 9.03 EST a second aircraft, American Airlines Flight 175, struck the South Tower. Sixty passengers and crew died on impact, again with numerous deaths occurring within the building as smoke and flames erupted from the burning fuel. A United Airlines Boeing 757 aircraft, identified as Flight 77, slammed into the Pentagon 34 minutes later, again killing all on board and wreaking death and havoc on the ground. America and the world watched the drama on television and feared the Apocalypse. But at 9.57, in the skies above Ohio, another drama was taking place.

United Airlines Flight 93, another Boeing 757, had taken off from Newark International Airport in New Jersey bound for San Francisco International. Forty minutes into the flight four dark-skinned hijackers forced their way into the cockpit and stabbed the pilot and second officer. One hijacker, a trained commercial pilot, took control of the autopilot and turned the commercial jetliner back eastwards. What might have seemed to the passengers as a 'routine' risk of air travel became part of a bigger plot as – un-monitored by the hijackers who concentrated their efforts and navigational interest in the cockpit – passengers and cabin crew were able to call home on their mobile phones and learn of the Twin Tower attacks. The only documented proof of what occurred after passengers had learned their probable fate comes from phone messages and cockpit voice recorders that recorded their actions. On learning of the two earlier suicide missions, passenger Tom Burnett told his wife: 'Don't worry, we're going to do something.' Another passenger, Todd Beamer, is clearly heard to shout, 'Are you ready? Let's roll!' as the passengers staged their fight for life by attacking the hijackers. A flight attendant told her husband that she had prepared boiling water to throw at the hijackers, who had already killed one passenger and fatally wounded the aircrew.

The black box flight recorder would later show that the hijacker piloting the aircraft had switched the yoke to manual control and made violent manoeuvres to throw the attacking passengers off balance. His efforts were in vain as Todd Beamer and Tom Burnett, along with the remaining 42 passengers and crew, put up a desperate fight for their lives. At 10.03, the Boeing 757 plummeted from the sky, turning on its side before plunging into a field close to the Stonycreek Township in Pennsylvania, leaving a crater 50 feet wide and 10 feet deep. All aboard, including the hijackers, died in the crash.

No one knows whether the hijackers' assigned target was the White House or Capitol Hill, but no doubt exists that the heroism and sacrifice of the passengers of Flight 93 saved lives on the ground and sent a signal to those who believed the West was compliant to an attack of such magnitude.

President Bush learned of the attacks on the Twin Towers as he read a book with schoolchildren at the Booker Elementary School in Sarasota, Florida. An immediate pre-planned operation to preserve the executive chain of command in the event of an attack on the US mainland swung into action. Meanwhile, National Security Adviser Condoleezza Rice was in the operations centre of the White House Situation Room attempting to gather together principal members of the National Security Council. Principal members of the NSC are the president, the vice president, the secretary of state, the secretary of the treasury, and the secretary of defence; additionally, the director of the CIA and the chairman of the Joint Chiefs of Staff play the role of statutory advisers to the Council. Rice was unable to make contact since 'Murphy's Law' contrived to place Secretary of State Colin Powell in Peru and Treasury Secretary Paul O'Neill in Japan. Henry Shelton, Chairman of the Joint Chiefs of Staff, was on his way to Europe for a NATO meeting. The only NSC members on American soil on that fateful morning were the president and vice president, CIA Director George Tenet, already in his car and heading for CIA headquarters, and Defence Secretary Donald Rumsfeld at the Pentagon, unaware of the death that would rain on the building in less than half an hour. There is no doubt that within that vital half hour mistakes were made that would give rise to conspiracy theories in the months and years ahead.

Finally the available executives began to gather. Vice President Dick Cheney had been propelled to the Presidential Emergency Centre two floors below the White House by Secret Service agents as American Airlines Flight 77 was tracked approaching the Pentagon. President Bush, meanwhile, was whisked back aboard Air Force One parked at Sarasota-Bradenton International Airport and flown to an 'undisclosed destination'. In the President's absence Dick Cheney now assumed control. Defence Secretary Rumsfeld meanwhile was assisting the evacuation of victims from the stricken Pentagon, hovered over by his anxious Pentagon Police bodyguard led by Aubrey Smith. There was a growing conviction that the United States was under attack but no one had collated enough evidence to know from whom. The principal executives of the country appeared to have splintered and lost cohesion at a vital time in the nation's history.

Indeed, the nation was under attack but not, as at first feared, from the forces of a sovereign nation with which it had long conducted affairs under a mantle of distrust. The

United States had been attacked by one man, whose diverse beliefs led him to view the country as a Great Satan bent on destroying the light of Islam in the East. His name was Osama bin Laden.

The 19 men acting on the orders of bin Laden and his al Qaeda terrorist organisation had infiltrated the USA at various points in the days leading up to the attacks. Their training had been extensive in seizing an aircraft in flight, controlling traumatised passengers, piloting a large jet liner – some had even registered in US flying schools to learn the basics of aviation and navigation. Each was a dedicated fundamentalist, ready and willing to die for their own and their leader's interpretation of Islam and the will of Allah. Within hours, agents of the Federal Bureau of Investigation had found in Portland the suitcase of Mohamed Atta, a 33-year-old Egyptian known for his links to al Qaeda.

As fate often decrees and every airline passenger is aware, luggage does not always travel with its owner. Atta's suitcase had missed the connection to Flight 11 and its contents revealed details of the day's attacks and the names of the 19 hijackers, together with the roles they were to play in the drama. German Intelligence and the US National Security Agency also picked up radio 'chatter' linking the attacks to Osama bin Laden. Bin Laden was known to the North Americans as a fierce Islamic extremist who had fought the Soviets during their invasion of Afghanistan at a time when the Soviets' *mujahedeen* opponents had been supplied with weapons and instructors by the US Central Intelligence Agency and the US Special Forces.

The air strike at the Pentagon had killed 184 passengers and victims on the ground but danger of a far greater proportion existed at the World Trade Center, where both towers burned fiercely at the level of impact. The North Tower had been struck between the 80th and the 101st floors, while the South Tower fire concentrated around the 84th level. The great height of the twin towers, both 110 storeys high, made it difficult for rescue and fire crews attempting to fight the conflagration and evacuate the buildings. On any working day, the towers were estimated to contain over 16,000 people working in their separate offices. Of special concern to the rescuers was the fate of those trapped above the levels of impact. In both towers many office workers had fled upwards to the roof, hoping for a helicopter evacuation, but the smoke and flames made such rescues impossible. Others, terrorised by the all-devouring flames advancing upon them, chose to jump from windows, their bodies raining on the roofs of buildings below or shattering blood and bone against the asphalt of the roads.

Many of those in the South Tower had been able to vacate the building following the North Tower strike and were safely in the streets below when the second aircraft struck the South Tower, but a rising panic in the North Tower, where only three staircases remained open for evacuation, meant rescue and fire crews struggled in the stairwell to pass injured and terrorised workers on their way down.

At 9.59 the South Tower creaked ominously and began to concertina downwards, floor after floor impacting on the floor below as the 110-storey structure collapsed like a house of cards. In the suburbs of Brooklyn and Jersey

City stunned New Yorkers saw the collapse and imagined they were witnessing the end of the world. A plume of smoke and ashes rose hundreds of feet in the air and a horizontal cloud of dust swept outwards on the ground as crowds fled before it, choking and coughing on the particles of grit and ash. Twenty-one minutes later, while fire crews worked within the building battling the smoke and heat to pull victims from the inferno, the North Tower collapsed in a similar fashion, further weakening the nearby Tower 7 of the World Trade complex. Tower 7 collapsed at 5.20 pm.

The total death toll would be calculated at 2605. Of these, 340 were members of the New York Fire Service and 72 were police officers who died attempting rescues in the stricken structures.

With the benefit of hindsight and now in possession of the attack plan, US federal agents began to trace the pre-September 11 movements of the dead hijackers under an operation named unimaginatively by the acronym PENTTBOM. Ominously, they discovered that the plot's chief organiser, Khalid Sheikh Mohammed, had gained approval for the attack from Osama bin Laden as early as autumn 1998. As the plot administrator, Mohammed selected the targets – it later emerged he had opted for an attack on the US Bank Tower in Los Angeles but had been overruled for whatever reason by the al Qaeda leader – and made travel arrangements for the hijackers. In 1999 Mohamed Atta, Marwan al-Shehhi, Ziad Jarrah, and Ramzi Binalshibh travelled from Hamburg to arrive in Afghanistan for selection and training. All were chosen as educated men who spoke English and had lived in the West.

Agents were also alarmed to discover that Atta, the plot leader, had changed his destination to go to the United States in June 2000, linking up with Hani Hanjour in December of that year, when they journeyed together to Arizona for casual, additional training at a flight school. Hanjour was an experienced commercial pilot and the man at the controls when Flight 11 flew into the North Tower. Marwan al-Shehhi had reached the USA a month earlier than Atta. Jarrah followed soon after. Binalshibh, a Yemeni, experienced some difficulty arranging a visa to the USA and returned to Hamburg where he acted as a liaison between Sheikh Mohammed and Atta, later meeting Atta in Madrid, Spain, to discuss final details. The other hijackers arrived in the USA in twos and threes in early 2001, and by late spring everyone was in place.

Later recriminations would focus on how members of an organisation already suspected of terrorism against the USA with the bombings of the *USS Cole* and the US embassies in Nairobi and Dar es Salaam, which together killed 306 locals and US nationals and injured more than 5000.

Post 9/11 would see the introduction of the Homeland Security Agency, repercussions on the Arab and Muslim communities, tighter border controls and visa requirements – but as a leading FBI agent put it, 'The horse had bolted, 3000 [sic] people died and we were just closing the door.'

Finally, the weight of evidence swung the scales towards al Qaeda and its leader Osama bin Laden, then quartered in Afghanistan. Bin Laden, a Saudi Arabian and the stepson of a wealthy Saudi builder, had become disenchanted with the first President Bush's efforts to control the Middle East oilfields through the 1991 intervention in Iraq's claim of Kuwait. During the Soviet invasion of the 1980s, Osama bin Laden was one of the key players in organising training camps for the foreign Muslim volunteers. The USA poured funds and arms into Afghanistan and, according to a Human Rights Watch report published in November 1998, by 1987, 65,000 tons of US-made weapons and ammunition a year were entering the war.

But three years before the attack on the World Trade Center and Pentagon, the disillusioned bin Laden had declared *jihad* – holy war – against the USA and signed a *fatwah* calling for the killing of American citizens wherever they should be found. Bin Laden had great wealth, through his family connections, and was known to have financed various acts of terrorism around the globe.

Five days after the fall of the World Trade Center, bin Laden made a declaration on the Arab TV station al-Jazeera denying any involvement in the 9/11 attacks, blaming 'individuals with their own motivation'. However, evidence of the terrorist leader's involvement would be unearthed by US forces following the subsequent invasion of Afghanistan in October 2001 by a US-led coalition.

Afghanistan had continued to wallow in a stew of fundamental Islamism until that fateful day in September 2001 when al Qaeda terrorists successfully attacked and destroyed the World Trade Center in New York. Suspicion had long been fostered in the West that the Taliban regime was providing facilities for al Qaeda training camps as well as a safe haven for the USA's arch-enemy Osama bin

Laden. Following the 9/11 attacks, the United States launched Operation Enduring Freedom, a military campaign to destroy the al Qaeda training camps inside Afghanistan. The US military also threatened to overthrow the Taliban government for refusing to hand over Osama bin Laden and several al Qaeda members, including suspected 9/11 architect Khalid Sheikh Mohammed. To achieve its ends to that effect the Bush administration made agreements with the Afghanistan *mujahedeen*, including forming the Northern Alliance, a militia recognised by NATO as a military arm of the Afghan Government.

In 2004 bin Laden himself acknowledged al Qaeda's planning of the attacks, and al-Jazeera TV broadcast a video in 2006 showing him shaking hands with three hijackers before they left for the USA. Khalid Sheikh Mohammed was arrested in Pakistan in 2003 and is currently being held in Guantánamo Bay, Cuba. He was due to go on trial in New York in 2010 for his part in the World Trade Center bombings.

In the immediate aftermath of that fateful day in September, the USA invoked special powers to ground all non-emergency civilian aircraft in the United States, Canada, and several other countries that came under the umbrella of the Security Control of Air Traffic and Air Navigation Aids, acronym SCATANA, a never-before-used US emergency plan to control Western hemisphere air traffic in the event of a national or international emergency. All international flights were denied access to American airspace by the Federal Aviation Authority, a protective move that caused chaos for tens of thousands of world travellers. The world's airports began to fill with the overflow of passengers from cancelled flights and many countries were forced to operate emergency measures to clear the backlog.

All nineteen hijackers died at the crash sites but their number is not included in the list of casualties. A total of 2605 persons died in the collapse of the World Trade Center towers, including firemen and police personnel. Eighty-seven passengers and crew died aboard American Airlines Flight 11 and 60 aboard United's Flight 175. One hundred and twenty-five were killed at the Pentagon, with 59 passengers and crew aboard AA Flight 77 dying with them. The heroic revolt by passengers on Flight 93 resulted in a death toll of 40, avoiding a much higher casualty figure if the aircraft had reached its intended target of either the White House or Capitol Hill. The total death toll was 2976 souls; 6000 people were injured. Nonetheless, the official total of deaths attributed to 9/11 has continued to rise over the intervening years as some of those who escaped death as the towers fell continue to succumb to the deadly effects of inhaled dust.

The site of the World Trade Center, now referred to as Ground Zero, is the place each year of a moving memorial service attended by the incumbent US president, his executive, and many of the families of the dead, when the name of each victim is read aloud. The damage to the area was extensive. In addition to the two main towers, many other surrounding buildings were either destroyed or so badly damaged as to warrant demolition. These included Towers 4, 5, 6, and 7, the Marriot World Trade Center Hotel, the World Financial Centre complex, and the St Nicholas Greek Orthodox Church. On the other side of Liberty Street directly opposite the stricken World Trade complex, the building occupied by the Deutsche Bank was condemned to demolition and the Borough of Manhattan Community College's Fiterman Hall on West Broadway was also demolished due to extensive damage.

Thus ended one of the most brutal crimes in the world's history, marking 11 September 2001 as the day that stands at the top of a woeful list for the most victims of an act of crime. The suspected architect is in custody and awaits trial. The master planner remains always a step ahead of the law.

CHAPTER 21

OKLAHOMA CITY BOMBING

Oklahoma, USA, 19 April 1995

'You learn how to handle killing in the military'
— Timothy McVeigh.

The path that led US militant Timothy McVeigh to murder 168 people in the bombing of the Oklahoma City Murrah Federal Building on 19 April 1995 began exactly two years before in Waco, Texas, when a standoff between federal agents and members of Branch Davidian cult ended in a bloody government massacre, the blame for which has never been fully established.

On 19 April 1993 the FBI moved in on the Branch Davidian compound, known as the Mount Carmel Centre, in Waco after months of reports that cult leader David Koresh had been abusing children and building up an arsenal of weapons. The Branch Davidian religious movement originated in the 1930s as an offshoot of the Church of the Seventh Day Adventists. Following a recent surge in reports, the Bureau of Alcohol, Tobacco, and Firearms, acronym

ATF, planned a raid on the compound, armed with warrants to search for illegal firearms. The first assault took place on 28 February 1993.

As an armed federal agent, clad in assault gear, climbed onto the roof of an outbuilding, a semi-automatic weapon opened up from inside the building and 7.62 mm rounds burst through the wall in an explosive flurry of debris, striking and killing the agent in the act. An exchange of gunfire developed into a fierce firefight that lasted nearly two hours. When the gunsmoke cleared, four ATF agents and five Branch Davidians lay dead.

For the next 51 days, aware of the focus of world media on the negotiations, the FBI attempted to end the conflict with negotiators but their efforts all met with failure. David Koresh was seen as Christ's reincarnation on earth by his followers and he was determined to end the standoff in either defeat for the bureaucracy against which his cult rebelled or martyrdom for the Branch Davidian members. He was to achieve the latter. During this period the FBI were able to facilitate the exit from the compound of a number of children and a few adults, but 84 men, women, and children remained.

Where armoured tanks and numerous bloody assaults had failed, the ATF leadership came up with an idea to end the siege by gassing the compound and sending its troops into the building while the Davidians were disabled. By this time the besieged Davidians were receiving moral support from civil rights groups across the country and the decision to use CS gas, a form of teargas, in a building with children, was strongly criticised. Nonetheless, the ATF plan was upheld by US Attorney General Janet Reno and at dawn on 19 April 1993 ATF armoured vehicles punched holes in the compound's wall and inserted canisters of CS gas in the hope of forcing the occupants out.

The Davidians held firm, although the choking atmosphere within the compound must have been close to unbearable. Some made suicidal charges out of the compound, firing as they came, and were shot down in retaliation. At noon, the wooden compound caught fire. Only nine Davidians managed to escape the blaze and were taken into custody. Attempts by fire services to control the blaze were met by gunfire and a sombre cordon eventually surrounded the compound to watch it burn. Seventy-five Davidians died within, either burned to death or from gunshots, many self inflicted or fired by parents to spare their children the agony of being burned alive. David Koresh was found among the dead, killed by a bullet to the head. Twenty-five of the dead were children and the world reeled in anger at the slaughter.

Many of the more militant felt the FBI, already under fire for its handling of the Ruby Ridge shoot out with the militant Weaver family in the previous year, had acted in a barbaric fashion and swore revenge. One of these was Timothy McVeigh, a 25-year-old ex-US Army veteran allied to militia movements in the USA. McVeigh was a staunch Republican, a member of the National Rifle Association, and a committed opponent of political bureaucracy and centralised government. Militants across the USA were still raw from the events at Ruby Ridge, a remote area of Idaho, where Randy Weaver, an ex-Green Beret, was shot to death by ATF federal agents along with his wife, a family friend, and Weaver's 13-year-old son while resisting arrest on the charge of selling a sawn-off shotgun.

McVeigh planned his revenge quietly. His chosen targets were the federal government, the FBI, and the Bureau of Alcohol, Tobacco, and Firearms, all of which he saw as responsible for the death toll at Waco. Ideally for McVeigh's plan of retribution, numerous federal agencies, including the ATF, had offices in the Alfred P Murrah Federal Building in downtown Oklahoma City. McVeigh's chosen day of retribution would be 19 April 1995, two years to the day of the Waco catastrophe.

Aware that he needed help to put his plan into action, McVeigh enlisted the aid of an older friend, 38-year-old fellow ex-US army veteran Terry Nichols who had served with McVeigh in the 1st Infantry Division. The prosecution would later allege that the bombing operation was funded by a US$60,000 robbery on the Arkansas home of gun dealer Roger Moore. Another accomplice, Michael Fortier, helped the pair move and sell the stolen guns and survey the Murrah Federal Building in preparation for the attack.

McVeigh's next move was to buy large amounts of the fertiliser, ammonium nitrate. The purchases took place in September 1994 and the materials were stored in a rented shed in Herington in neighbouring Kansas, where Nichols lived. Together with other ingredients stolen from a Kansas quarry, the nitrate/fuel-oil bomb was prepared and made ready for detonation. Ammonium nitrate acts as an oxidising agent to feed the explosion and needs extreme heat to detonate. This would be supplied by Tovex gel, a dynamite substitute, easier than the latter to transport and handle. The Tovex had been stolen with other items from the quarry and would necessitate the initiation of a fuse to start the explosion. The man with a proverbial match would be McVeigh.

The planning and building of the Oklahoma City bomb reveals a marked knowledge of blast dynamics that only hints at the vast array of underground intelligence available to those who turn to terrorism against the institutions and elected governments of the world. The McVeigh bomb was made up of 50,000 pounds of explosive grade ammonium nitrate fertiliser and 17 bags of ammonium nitrate mixed with diesel oil, 165 US gallons of liquid nitromethane – a volatile, aromatic solvent used in dry cleaning that often causes suitcases containing dry-cleaned clothes to be opened by airport security. There were also quantities of Tovex blasting gel and dual detonating devices of shock tubes, which employ a collision of high and low pressure gases to generate heat, and the more unsophisticated cannon fuse, ignited by a match or pistol shot. Indeed, McVeigh arranged for the possibility of being discovered while still in the driving seat and was prepared to ignite a cannon fuse under where he would be sitting by firing a pistol, and losing his own life in the process.

On the morning of 19 April, McVeigh drove a rented truck, loaded two days earlier with the help of Terry Nichols, with 5000 pounds of the ammonium nitrate mixture, and parked in the parking lot in front of the Murrah Federal Building. The time was 8.58 am and most of the employees were already at their desks, those who were parents having dropped their children off at the daycare centre located on the first floor of the building immediately above where McVeigh now parked the truck. McVeigh left the keys in the vehicle and casually exited the cab after setting the three-minute shock tube timer that protruded into the cab from the rear through another hole drilled behind the passenger seat. He loped across the parking lot and disappeared down an alley across North West Fifth Street.

The explosion occurred at 9.02 am and the swathe of damage was enormous, knocking out three massive support columns of the Murrah Building and destroying or damaging 324 buildings within a 16-block radius, injuring more than 680 people. In the rubble of the collapsed nine-storey building lay 168 dead, including the small bodies of 19 children, the youngest of whom was only three months old. A case study of the building collapse by the National Institute of Standards and Technology showed that the blast, which was heard 55 miles away as a distant, echoing thud, and subsequent collapse of the building had destroyed 58,100 square feet of the building's 137,000 square feet of floor space, a destruction ration of 42 per cent. The parking of the truck-bomb close to the main supporting pillars had been a stroke of unconscious fate that was to be recorded as the largest terrorist attack in the United States until 11 September 2001.

Of the dead, 99 worked for the federal government. All those who survived were found during the first day – the last survivor of the blast, a 15-year-old female, was pulled from the wreckage of the basement at 7.00 pm – but the search continued for nearly three weeks. After days of combing the rubble, the official total of deaths stood at 168 and rescuers were left wondering who was the owner of an unmatched leg, all that was left of victim 169. The rescue work went on, with civilian agencies, National Guardsmen and individual volunteers searching through the debris, assisted by sniffer dogs. Occasional calls for silence rang out when a whimper was heard from below the searchers' feet.

Some victims were so badly trapped by crushed limbs mangled under concrete girders that these were often amputated without anaesthetic for fear of inducing coma in the victim. Another problem facing rescuers was releasing victims who had lain with limbs trapped under pressure from above. In these cases, a condition can occur known as Bywaters' Syndrome, first recognised during the London Blitz of the Second World War, in which toxins are leached into the blood by the damaged muscles, which build up in the trapped limb until release of pressure when they surge into the circulation, with fatal results. Given that the removal of victims at risk from Bywaters' Syndrome could not be effected without strict medical supervision, further rescues were often hampered by the need to leave some victims in situ until additional medical help arrived.

The search was further delayed by the discovery of what was believed to be a second bomb, and streets around the site and the site itself were mandatorily evacuated by police, despite the unwillingness of searchers to leave the site. Eventually the very real-looking threat turned out to be an inactive TOW missile used as a training aid for federal agents. With the survivors rescued and hospitalised within ten hours, the searchers knew they couldn't relax; attending to the dead would take much longer.

A temporary morgue was set up in the debris-strewn car parking lot and 16 forensic investigators used fingerprinting, dental scans, and DNA testing to identify victims, many of whom were beyond visual recognition. The recovery of the dead continued until just after midnight on 5 May, with the bodies of three of the victims still unaccounted for. The decision to stop was taken in view of the instability of the upper floors after a nurse working at the scene had been killed when struck on the head by falling debris, and other injuries were sustained by searchers.

But the stroke of fate that had led McVeigh to place the truck bomb in the situation where it would do the most damage did not benefit the bomber after the explosion. Within 90 minutes of leaving the city he was pulled over by a Highway Patrol officer for driving his eight-year-old yellow Mercury Marquis without a vehicle licence plate. A routine search of his vehicle discovered the unregistered Glock 21 semi-automatic with which he had been prepared to initiate the bomb, and McVeigh was arrested. As he languished in his cell, news of the Oklahoma City bombing was circulated by the news media and suspicious officers began to examine the background of their latest prisoner.

The story gradually unfolded of McVeigh's anti-establishment activities and his affiliation to militia movements. The car in which he had been arrested also offered stark evidence of McVeigh's political leanings with an envelope carrying anti-government documents together with a bumper sticker with the Samuel Adams' homily 'When the government fears the people there is freedom. When the people fear the government there is tyranny' hidden in the glove compartment. McVeigh wore a T-shirt emblazoned with the words of presidential assassin John

Wilkes Booth, '*Sic semper tyrannis*' ('Thus always to tyrants') as he leapt to the stage of the Ford Theatre after shooting President Lincoln. The most damning find was a business card that McVeigh attempted to hide before being handcuffed. The card bore the address of a Wisconsin military surplus store and on the back in McVeigh's handwriting were the fateful words: 'TNT at $5 a stick. Need more'.

McVeigh was also found to be on the FBI list of nationals with grudges, imagined or otherwise, against the federal government. FBI Special Agent in Charge, Weldon L Kennedy, questioned McVeigh at length and soon after the bomber's interrogation Terry Nichols surrendered himself for questioning, and Michael Fortier and his wife Lori were arrested. Michael Fortier and his wife, who had witnessed conversations between Nichols, McVeigh, and her husband, later turned State's Evidence in exchange for a plea bargain to escape a possible death penalty.

A whimsical note of graveside humour entered the court proceedings with the charge against McVeigh for the murder of the owner of the unmatched left leg. McVeigh's leading defence counsel Stephen Jones seized upon the uncertainty of the leg's owner by claiming it could have belonged to an unknown mystery bomber whom he suggested was responsible for the explosion at the Murrah Federal Building. Stephen Jones's claim was dismissed by the prosecutors, who pointed out that eight victims had been buried without a left leg. Although at first thought to be that of a man, the leg was finally identified by a relative as belonging to Lakesha Levy, a female Air Force member who died in the bombing. A dilemma existed in that Levy had been buried with two legs, albeit that the left leg was detached and had been possibly chosen at random by a tidy-minded mortuary attendant. Levy's coffin was reopened and her own leg replaced the one previously buried with her. Unfortunately, a DNA test of the recovered limb was impossible since the original leg had been embalmed along with Levy's corpse before burial. Thus an orphan leg remains unidentified. A claim from its original owner is deemed unlikely.

The investigation into Timothy McVeigh and his accomplices continued. Delving through the wreckage of the truck, investigators were able to match it to a Ryder Truck Hire company in Junction City, where the owner of the franchise helped produce a police artist sketch that was remarkably similar to McVeigh's thin, drawn features. Other witnesses recalled the driver of a large yellow Ryder truck stopping overnight in a roadside motel en route to Oklahoma City on the night prior to the explosion. The motel register was signed by McVeigh, using his real name but a false address.

McVeigh was tried on the unlicensed weapon charge on 21 April at a court in Perry, Oklahoma, near where he was apprehended. He was immediately rearrested by FBI agents as he left the court. Meanwhile, Terry Nichols had walked into a police station and turned himself in. In a search of Nichols's home, investigators found blasting caps and a residue of ammonium nitrate along with tools used to break into a storage shed at the quarry. There were also books on bomb-making and propaganda material distributed by the National Alliance, a radical, neo Nazi, white separatist political organisation founded by the late William Luther Pierce and located at the family's compound in West Virginia.

The search also yielded a hand-drawn map of Oklahoma City, indicating the Murrah Federal Building and the spot where McVeigh's car had been left to facilitate his getaway after initiating the truck bomb. Nichols was held in custody, charged with acting as an accessory to murder committed during a terrorist act. The death penalty loomed.

James Nichols, Terry's brother, was arrested a week later but released after four weeks of interrogation for lack of evidence. McVeigh's sister, Jennifer, who had somehow committed the unremarkable crime of sending live ammunition to her brother through the mail, was granted immunity in exchange for testifying against him. Finally, the official investigation was over and authorities were satisfied that Timothy McVeigh and his accomplices had acted alone, without the prompting of external organisations such as the Middle East terrorists who had bombed the North Tower of the World Trade Center in 1993.

McVeigh went to trial in Denver, Colorado, on 24 April 1997 after federal judge Richard Matsch ruled that public opinion was so aroused that the defendant would not receive a fair trial in Oklahoma. Nearly 150 witnesses were called by the prosecution to give evidence of McVeigh's hatred of the government and his desire to take militant action against all federal authority. Prosecution witnesses included Michael Fortier and his wife Lori and McVeigh's sister Jennifer. Fortier's plea bargain didn't exclude a charge against him for failing to inform the authorities of the intended bombing, for which he would later receive a 12-year sentence and a fine of US$75,000 but did include immunity for Lori who had forged a driving licence for McVeigh to use in the truck hire.

Throughout the trial McVeigh continuously declared his hatred for the workings of federal government and his belief that liberty would only come about through the militia movement. The militia movement in the USA is an unorganised political organisation based on quasi military aims and the right of the people to bear arms as enshrined in the Second Amendment of the American Constitution. It is the belief of adherents to the militia that the US government seeks to erode that right for fear of armed insurrection by the gradual imposition of laws such as the Brady Bill, signed into federal law by President Clinton in 1993. The Brady Bill makes the provision that a background check must take place on a would-be purchaser of a firearm or in the case of an application to carry a concealed handgun.

McVeigh's defence counsel, Stephen Jones, often clashed with his client in his presentation of mitigating circumstances aimed at sparing McVeigh the death sentence. While not proud of his act – McVeigh openly regretted the deaths of children from the Federal Building's Day Care Centre and said he 'might have changed his target had he known of the presence of the children' – the bomber insisted that the blame for the bombing lay at the door of Congress and its 'stifling laws and taxation' of and against the American people. McVeigh's chosen defence was that he had acted out of necessity to prevent further outrages by the FBI, a tool of federal government, such as the Waco and Ruby Ridge massacres of American citizens. Neither man's presentation of mitigation won and on 2 June McVeigh was found guilty of 11 counts of murder and conspiracy. He was executed by lethal injection at the US penitentiary in Terre Haute, Indiana, nine days later. His execution was the first federal execution in 38 years.

Terry Nichols narrowly escaped the death sentence when he was found guilty of eight counts of involuntary manslaughter – smacking of a deal with the prosecution – and conspiring to build a weapon of mass destruction. He was sentenced to life without parole. As the vengeful relative of a murdered victim declared, 'They hung Saddam Hussein and they couldn't even find his WMDs – this motherfucker helped put one in a truck...' Nichols was in fact found guilty in a later trial of 161 counts of first degree murder but a deadlocked jury couldn't resolve the issue of the death sentence. Presiding judge Steven W Taylor finally sentenced him to 161 consecutive life sentences without parole. Nichols is serving his sentences in the ADX Florence Maximum Penitentiary in Florida.

Michael Fortier served ten-and-a-half years of his 12-year sentence before being released into the Witness Protection Program with a new identity.

A national memorial and museum honouring the victims, survivors, and rescuers of the Oklahoma City bombing was established on 9 October 1997 and dedicated on the fifth anniversary of the disaster on 19 April, 2000. It is the largest memorial of its kind on US soil.

CHAPTER 22

THE 7 JULY LONDON BOMBINGS

London, England, 7 July 2005

'White people are trash'
    – Germaine Lindsay, one of the four suicide bombers.

Commonly cited estimates of the Muslim world population in 2009 ranged from 1 billion to 1.8 billion. Up to 40 countries are of a Muslim majority and Arabs account for around 20 per cent of all Muslims worldwide. South Asia and South-East Asia contain the most populous Muslim countries, with Indonesia, India, Pakistan, and Bangladesh each having more than 100 million adherents to the faith. According to US government figures, in 2006 there were 20 million Muslims in China. In the Middle East, the non-Arab countries of Turkey and Iran have the largest Muslim majority of the region. On the African continent, Egypt and Nigeria have the most populous Muslim communities. Islam is the second largest religion after Christianity in many European countries.

Western-led invasions into the Middle East, including those of Iraq and Afghanistan, have led to resentment among the predominantly Muslim populations in much the same way that the British military in Northern Ireland in the 1970s suffered an increase in attacks from the Provisional IRA following a particularly successful operation against the Republicans; the Republicans, meanwhile, enjoying a surge in recruitment. Familiar to all Muslims is the call to *jihad,* which means to strive or struggle in the way of God and is considered the Sixth Pillar of Islam by a minority of Sunni Muslim authorities. In its broadest sense, *jihad* is classically defined as exerting one's utmost power, efforts, endeavours, or ability in contending with an object of evil disposition. Dependent on the object being a visible enemy, *jihad* commonly refers to military action.

Immigration, naturalisation, and burgeoning lessons of hate by reactionary imams protected under Europe's faltering Human Rights legislation by the very authorities that they preach to overthrow, has brought the war to the capitals of the West. On 7 July 2005 London became the latest victim.

Between 8.50 and 9.47 am on that Thursday morning in the height of British summer, three explosions ripped through three packed London Underground passenger trains in less than three minutes. Within an hour, at 9.47 precisely, a fourth bomb tore the roof off a double-decker bus in Tavistock Square in fashionable Bloomsbury. In total 52 people died, mostly commuters on their way to work, and more than 900 workers and visitors were injured. All four bombers died in the explosions, which were caused by primitive, home-made devices employing commercial organic peroxide to initiate the explosions.

The first bomb, which was detonated on an eastbound Circle Line train travelling between Aldgate and Liverpool Street, was exploded by Shehzad Tanweer, a 22-year-old Anglo-Pakistani from Leeds, as were two of the other bombers. Seven people were killed instantly along with the bomber and 171 were injured. The second explosion occurred on the westbound Circle Line between Edgware Road and Paddington and was detonated by Mohammad Siddique Khan, a teaching assistant from Beeston in Leeds.

At 8.53 the rear of the first carriage of a train on the southbound Piccadilly Line, travelling between King's Cross and Russell Square on its journey out to London's Heathrow Airport, was ripped apart, damaging the second carriage and spreading limbs and body parts across the track as the jam-packed commuters were blown apart, their blood spattering on the walls of the tunnel. The third bomber, 19-year-old Jamaican Germaine Lindsay from Huddersfield, died amidst the gore of his victims. Lindsay had taken the unofficial name of Abdullah Shaheed Jamal on converting to Islam.

London's emergency services stood stunned by the blasts, with unconfirmed reports claiming seven detonations had occurred at different locations. Asians and dark-skinned men were stopped and searched by police, and Indians and Pakistanis going about their legitimate business in Central London were viewed with suspicion. And yet more horror was to come.

Just before 9.45 am, in Tavistock Square to the north of the blood bath on the Underground, 18-year-old Hasib

Hussain, who had hesitated earlier and was now unable to enter the Underground due to the closures caused by the earlier bombings, boarded a number 30 bus picking up stranded commuters at Baker Street Station. Hussain took his rucksack up to the upper deck and sat in the rear seats. Passengers who survived the blast would later recall the 'olive-skinned' young man who was nervously checking his bag on the floor at his feet. Others remember only a loud 'bang' that stunned passers-by and the birds in the tree-lined square to silence before the screams began.

Thirteen people, including Hussain, died in the wreckage of the bus. The injuries of those who survived were described to the author as 'awesome' by a doctor working in the offices of the British Medical Association in Woburn Place, near where the blast occurred. One screaming victim had lost both legs below the knees, just bones devoid of flesh protruding from beneath the joints. Another had been decapitated by flying wreckage, the detached head found in the road some distance from the wrecked bus. Others had lost arms or legs. Those amputees who survived did so due to the traumatic nature of the amputation, in which a torn artery will contract on itself and stem bleeding. A clean-cut artery will remain open and the victim will rapidly bleed to death.

The scene in Tavistock Square was now reminiscent of the London Blitz more than 60 years before. The smoking hull of the wrecked bus had virtually been blown in half by the force of the explosion, the roof being completely detached and landing 20 feet away. Miraculously, the driver of the bus, 50-year-old Greek immigrant George Psaradakis, survived the explosion along with passengers occupying the front portion of both decks. The explosion had ripped the roof upwards and forwards, showering the occupants of the upper front seats with glass and metal but the real force of the explosion had been projected downwards. No one at the rear of the bus survived.

Psaradakis recalls that he had just started another journey from Marble Arch to Stratford when his control alerted him to 'a problem on the Underground' and to expect heavy loads of diverted train commuters. At Baker Street, where hundreds of passengers denied access to the Underground queued up for surface transport, his bus quickly filled up. Among the boarding passengers was Hussain, now determined to carry out his thwarted message of hate and join his dead colleagues in their martyrdom.

Many passengers were agitated at the delays and slow-moving traffic and unconsciously saved their own lives by jumping from the bus to join the walking crowds on the pavements. Police diversions around Euston forced Psaradakis to take his bus to Tavistock Square, where he stopped to ask directions from a traffic warden. 'As I pulled away, the bus exploded behind me,' he recalled. 'It was horrible. My bus had been full of young men and women, laughing and chatting on their mobile phones, full of life. Now there was only death and cries of pain.' George Psaradakis eventually returned to work and still drives a number 30 bus but he admits to an attack of the shakes whenever he nears Tavistock Square, which was a diversion on the day of the bombing and is not on the official number 30 route. Every Sunday he lights a candle in his local church for the victims.

Of the four suicide bombers, the oldest and assumed leader of the cell was Mohammad Siddique Khan. Like Hussain and Tanweer, he was British-born to Pakistani parents, having entered the world in St James University Hospital in Leeds on 20 October 1974. He grew up around the Leeds area and married an Indian Muslim, Hasina Patel, in 2001. After leaving Leeds University, where he had met his future wife, Khan worked at a primary school in Leeds, teaching children of immigrant families and helping them to adjust to life in their new host country. According to friends and colleagues Khan never discussed his religious or political beliefs and avoided comments on the situation in Iraq or Afghanistan. Nonetheless, he was a committed Muslim and regularly attended the Stratford Street mosque in Beeston, Leeds.

Shehzad Tanweer, younger by eight years, had been born in Bradford in 1982, again of Pakistani parentage, and was described by friends as a political moderate. Just after his second birthday his family moved from Bradford to Leeds where he eventually attended Leeds University. Tanweer was known to have travelled to Pakistan in 2004 to attend a course of Islamic studies at a *madrasah* – one of a number of religious schools run by imams where students study Islam and the teachings of the Koran. *Madrasahs* are reported to be the point of supply for Pakistani recruits to the Taliban-inspired insurgent forces in Afghanistan. Neighbours in Colwyn Road, Leeds, remember a slightly-built young man who occasionally worked in his parents' fish-and-chip shop. Tanweer also attended the Stratford Street mosque in Beeston where he probably met Khan and Hussain.

The third bomber, Germaine Lindsay, was born in Jamaica, which he last saw at age five when his family emigrated to the UK in 1990, finally settling in Dalton, a suburb of Huddersfield. After leaving secondary education at Rawthorpe High School he eventually found work as a carpet fitter and moved south to Aylesbury in Buckinghamshire. Of all the bombers, Lindsay had a further motive for his actions on 7 July 2005. He hated white people and was a confirmed racist, known to police for his drug dealing and street violence, who had been dealing in heroin and crack cocaine since the age of 14. One reformed customer recalls him telling her: 'All white people are trash and I'm going to get all of them on drugs to kill them off.' It is clear that Germaine Lindsay saw his conversion to Islam at the age of 15 as a rejection of the West and his host country, a rejection and deep-rooted hatred that would lead him to commit mass murder four years later.

Following his conversion Lindsay shunned old colleagues in the drug trade and concentrated on the anti-establishment rhetoric of his new religion, often being seen in the company of Abdullah el-Faisal, formerly Trevor Forrest, a Jamaican Muslim who preached at the Brixton mosque in South London.

Despite his youth, Lindsay married twice: first to Irish-born Aoife Nadiyah Molloy, lasting eight days before he deserted his young bride and divorced her to marry another Irish woman, Samantha Lewthwaite, who was also a teenage convert to Islam. Lewthwaite bore him two children, the second born two months after his death. Following the London bombings, his wife would go on record insisting that her husband's mind had been warped by radicals, including Abdullah el-Faisal, who had also studied abroad for seven years at a *madrasah* in Saudi Arabia.

El-Faisal, who gave lectures to study groups throughout

the UK, may well have been the link between Lindsay and the Leeds cell. Certainly his lectures, which were recorded on tape and sold at specialist bookshops, would have been known to Khan, Tanweer, and Hussain. El-Faisal was denounced by the Brixton mosque administration in 1993 for his inflammatory preaching and deported back to Jamaica in 2007 – two years too late for the victims of the London bombings – after serving four years of a nine-year sentence imposed at the Old Bailey in 2003 for urging his listeners to kill Jews, Hindus, and Americans. He would later, probably assessing the mood of the Islamic world towards radicals, condemn the London bombings as 'immoral'.

The fourth bomber, the reluctant Hasib Hussain, was the youngest of the group, and the youngest of four children. Born in Leeds and raised in the suburb of Holbeck, Hussain was tall for his age and looked up to by his peers for his prowess on the sports field. He was a member of both the Holbeck Hornets FC and the Holbeck cricket team, described by his classmates and teachers at the South Leeds High School as 'a slow, gentle giant'.

As a youth growing up in the multicultural society of Leeds, Hussain did not demonstrate any particular religious interest until his return from a visit to his parents' homeland of Pakistan in 2003, after which he started wearing the traditional Muslim dress of the *sirwal* and tunic, grew a beard, and made the *hajj*, the traditional pilgrimage of Muslims to Mecca. Around the time of his conversion, he met Khan and Tanweer through his attendance at the Stratford Street mosque in Beeston. Along with Tanweer he was also a regular visitor to the Hamara Youth Access Point, a drop-in centre for Muslim teens in Leeds, which is operated by an Islamic charity and partly funded by the UK government. Acting as a youth mentor at the centre was Mohammad Siddique Khan, the probable recruiter of the Leeds cell destined to carry out the London bombings.

It is an anomaly, not unfamiliar in contemporary Britain, that the Hamara Youth Access Point, known familiarly as Hyap, received grants from Westminster totalling over £1 million, funding an Islamic bookshop that sold, among its more traditional ware, political videos and DVDs containing graphic footage from Iraq, Afghanistan, and the West Bank, claimed by British Intelligence to form part of anti-Western propaganda.

Each year, on 7 July in the village of Chak 477 in Pakistan's Punjab region, Pakistan-based relatives of Shehzad Tanweer hold a celebration in which prayers are said for the soul of the 'martyr Shehzad' and food is distributed to the mourners. A large empty grave in nearby Samundari cemetery bearing Tanweer's name is also visited to offer prayers for his soul. There is no suggestion that any of Tanweer's British family members have ever attended the ceremony.

AFTERWORD

Reading the contents of this book may give the feeling that the world is not a safe place for the law-abiding citizen, always bearing in mind that criminals risk death due to their profession rather more than office clerks or shop assistants. The risk of deadly attack is always, of course, dictated by where one lives. According to the grandly named Seventh United Nations Survey of Crime Trends and Operations of Criminal Justice Systems' list of 52 countries, the country currently at the top of the worldwide 'hit' list is Colombia, with 26,539 homicides in the survey period between 1998 and 2000. The USA is 24th , with 16,204, and the United Kingdom, at 46th place, managed a modest 1201. According to the UN, the place where you're least likely to meet an assassin is Qatar, where only one murder was committed in the three-year period of the survey. Nonetheless, there is no doubt that the world is becoming more wicked day-by-day, so these statistics are by no means an indicator that it can't happen to us. It can and infrequently does, and always when we least expect it.

In my time as an investigative crime journalist I have witnessed the unspeakable limits to which men and women will go when inflamed by anger, passion, greed, or all three. It's a wicked, wicked world, so be careful out there...